Chasing Butterflies

Mary Weeks Millard

© Day One Publications 2016

First printed 2016

ISBN 978-1-84625-517-5

All Scripture quotations are from the **New International Version** 1984
Copyright © 1973, 1978, 1984

Published by Day One Publications
Ryelands Road, Leominster, HR6 8NZ

TEL 01568 613 740 FAX 01568 611 473

email—sales@dayone.co.uk

UK web site—www.dayone.co.uk

Cover design by ELK Design

Printed by TJ International

Dedication

To Sam, Megan and Emily.

I hope you enjoy this new book and it helps you to grow in your faith.

Acknowledgements

To Tirzah and Chris Jones and all the staff at DayOne who have helped and encouraged me. To my friends who have taken the time to read this book and comment on it. Last, but by no means least, to Malcolm, my dear husband, who always supports and encourages me in every part of my life.

Chapter One

E rnest was so excited! The long summer holidays had arrived at last. His trunk was packed and the porter had carried it to the front hall where it was waiting to be taken to the railway station. Soon he would be on his way home!

It wasn't that Ernest didn't like his boarding school, Wheelie Hall, but he really wanted to see his family again and have fun with his sisters through the six weeks' break. He would miss his schoolmates, especially Simon, who was his best friend, but he was glad that lessons and exams were over for a while. When he returned in September, he would be entering the senior section of the school, and that meant he would have a better chance of getting into some of the school clubs and societies. He so wanted to join the Natural History Society. Already he longed to be an explorer like his father!

It was a bright sunny day and soon Ernest, along with several other boys, was sitting in the horse-drawn omnibus which had been hired to take them to the railway station in order to catch the London bound train. On the platform the boys looked down the line to see who could get the first glimpse of the steaming monster which would take them to the beautiful, newly-built St Pancras station. There was so much hustle, bustle and noise when the train arrived! The porters put the trunks into the guard's van while the boys found seats. The smell of steam and coal was exciting, and no one seemed to mind the fact that bits of soot flew into their eyes and up their noses! The boys began to chant together,

No more Latin, no more French,
No more sitting on the old school bench

and they raised their school caps up and down as they chanted. Eventually, they stopped and settled down into their seats.

The journey took about two hours, but everyone was chattering about the things which they hoped to do in the long holiday. Matron had packed each boy a packet of sandwiches which they soon ate with great relish even though it was not long since breakfast. Every station at which they stopped was a place of interest. Most of them had gardens alongside the platform and vied with each other to have the prettiest flowers. Not all the boys took interest in the flowers, but Ernest looked out of the window at every stop to see if there were any butterflies flying around. His father was not only an explorer but also a butterfly hunter. Ernest so wanted to follow in his footsteps and one day go to some exotic country and discover a butterfly which no one before him had ever found!

Simon looked at his friend's eager face.

"I suppose you'll spend most of the hols looking for butterflies and moths?" he commented.

"I hope so," answered Ernest. "What about you, Si, have you any plans?"

"I think Pater and Mater are planning to take us all to Switzerland. Pater says it's to improve our French, but he just loves the mountains and lakes. He gets a good break from Parliament so we can go climbing and exploring together."

"That's what I miss," said Ernest a little sadly. "Father goes away for years at a time and we hear very little from him. He's been in the Congo for well over a year now, and we have no idea when he will get home. Mother does all she can to keep our spirits up, but it must be hard for her. 'A boy needs his father around'—she is always saying that."

The train screeched to a halt, and the boys were distracted from looking out of the window and watched the fireman take water from a large tank at the side of the track through a huge hose. He then steamed up the engine once more, and they continued puffing their way on their journey, all through the countryside and the suburbs of London, until eventually they pulled into St Pancras station with all its ornate brass arches and glass dome. This always gave Ernest a thrill.

The boys rushed out of the train and went to the guard's van, where porters were taking out their school trunks and also where they were to meet the people collecting them. Some boys were met by their parents, but others like Ernest were met by household staff who had been sent to collect them.

Brown, the footman, whom the children affectionately called

'Brownie', was waiting as usual for Ernest. He had already paid a porter to carry the trunk outside the station to where a horse-drawn cab was waiting.

"Up you get, young master," said Brownie, giving Ernest a hand up into the cab. Then, having secured the trunk safely at the back, he climbed in and instructed the 'cabbie' to drive them to Addiscombe, a lovely little village on the outskirts of Croydon, which was an exciting new housing area in South London.

When they arrived at Myrtle House on the Upper Addiscombe Road, the 'cabbie' was paid and quite a reception committee was waiting for Ernest.

His ten-year-old sister, Elizabeth-Ann, whom almost everybody called 'Libby-Ann', was jumping up and down with excitement, but her governess Miss Austerberry was trying to make her behave in the way that a Victorian young lady should! Next to her stood his little sister, Elspeth, with the nursery maid Polly holding her hand. Cook was Brownie's wife, and she beamed and said, "Welcome home, young Master Ernest."

His mother, looking as beautiful as ever and very elegant in a grey silk dress, came forward and gave her son a hug and then more formally shook his hand.

"See, we are all here to welcome you home. Everyone has been in a state of excitement since breakfast! Now come along in and we will all have lunch. Brownie will take your trunk to your room. Next year you will be old enough to come home on the branch line to Addiscombe Station, though I know Brownie will still want to come and meet you. He loves his trips to London when he collects you and Father when he arrives home!"

As Ernest entered the front door of their large Victorian double-fronted house, he paused and asked his mother, "How is Father? Have you had any news? Will he be home soon? Has he found any rare species?" His mother laughed. "One question at a time, Ernest. That's all I can cope with! We did have a letter just a week ago, and since you were coming home I didn't write to you to tell you his news. You can read the letter for yourself after luncheon."

Once everyone was inside, Ernest ran upstairs to his room. It was so great to have a room of his own even though it was still on the top 'nursery' floor. Sometimes, when he was in the school dormitory which held ten boys, he longed for his own space.

His room had a dormer window which looked out on to the road, and he loved watching all the horse-drawn vehicles which passed on their way to and from Croydon. All his books and toys were just as he had left them, though not a speck of dust was to be seen, so the housemaid, Constance, must have done her work well. It was good to be home!

In a few minutes Ernest had poured some water from the big jug on his washstand into the basin and washed the soot from his hands and face. Steam trains were exciting, but they did make the passengers very sooty! Then he took off his school uniform, folded it up and found his old sailor suit in his wardrobe. He knew he had almost grown out of it, but it was his favourite suit for playing around in and he intended to do a lot of that through the holiday!

The gong sounded loudly, and he rushed downstairs to the dining room. The girls followed him. Usually they ate in the day nursery, but this was a special day and they were to eat luncheon in the dining room with their mother. Libby-Ann wanted to tell him all her news, and Elspeth was chattering away as well. They were a happy family and glad to be together again.

"It would be perfect if Father were here too!" said Libby-Ann, and everyone agreed.

After they had eaten, Ernest was handed the letter from their Father.

"One of the other members of the expedition was travelling to South Africa and sent this letter with the captain of a ship bound for England. It was wonderful to have some news again," explained their mother. "I think you will manage to read his writing without too much difficulty. Read aloud the first two pages, then hand it back to me, for the rest is personal."

Ernest took the letter and began to read in a clear voice so that even Elspeth could understand.

My dear Belinda and precious children,

I am so sorry that you have heard so little from me; tomorrow one of our expedition members has to go by river steamer down the Congo River and then trek onwards to South Africa. If he makes it safely to Port Elizabeth, then he will get this letter on a ship bound for England.

This is a difficult trip for us in many ways because so many of our party have been sick with malaria and yellow fever. Two have died from the latter disease. Sometimes we traverse through thick jungle and at other times through savannah where many wild animals roam. It is magnificent to see them!

I love the giraffes; they are so tall and elegant! I wish you could all see them. At night we have fires burning near our encampment and guards watching over us because of the lions. Not all of them are dangerous, but there is always the threat that one might be a 'man-eater'. The chimpanzees are always around us and are very cheeky! They are fascinated by everything, so we have to watch that they don't steal our belongings. The reptile hunters in our expedition get very excited when they find snakes. I have to be honest and say that I don't feel the same.

Maybe during this summer holiday you could all go to the London Zoological Gardens. It would be a good expedition for you to make. You can see some of the animals which I am seeing here in the Congo.

Keep up your butterfly hunting, children. I will want to see your collections when I eventually come home. I am finding so many species here in the Congo. They are very beautiful, and my collection and drawings are growing. I often have to make the drawings during the night-time using a paraffin lantern. The light from this lantern also draws all sorts of moths and other insects into the tent. I spend a lot of my time when I am in here on my mattress underneath a mosquito net. Those little insects are the cause of so much illness amongst us and the native people here. The quinine tablets we take seem to make us all feel a bit sick, and our skin always has a yellowish tinge. We will end up looking more like Chinese than English people!

Several of the expedition are deeply committed Christians, and I have begun to read and study the Bible with them. Although I have always attended church and said my prayers and taught you all to do the same, it has

11

never meant anything very much to me. It has always been a duty. Now I am learning more about Jesus, who he is and why he came to earth. It is exciting, and I want to encourage you to read your Bibles and pray and find out about Jesus for yourself. All around us we see the Congolese people living in great fear of evil spirits and afraid of upsetting their ancestors. I am beginning to understand why missionaries come and live in countries like the Congo to bring the good news that Jesus came to forgive and save us.

Soon we will be exploring the volcanic mountains. It will be unexplored territory and may be very dangerous. We will be in the places where the gorillas live and also the pygmy people. It may be impossible for me to get any news home to you all for a very long time. Please do not forget to pray for me that I will really get to know more about Jesus and how to be a disciple and follow him, also that I may be kept safe and one day return home to you all, along with many, many butterflies.

Meanwhile, my dearest children, be well-behaved for your mother and those who care for you. Ernest, work hard at school, and Elizabeth-Ann, learn your lessons well with your governess. Both of you be kind to Elspeth and help her with her nursery learning. Remember what I said about getting to know Jesus—that will be the most important lesson of your lives.

There are many exciting things happening in Britain just now, including many, many new inventions and developments. Also, lots of new places are being discovered throughout the world. Learn about them! Be curious! Be glad you are alive while our wonderful Queen Victoria is sovereign. Pray for her in her grief over dear Prince Albert's death.

I have one other request. It may seem a very strange one, but living here in such a remote place is teaching me many things. My sister, Ernestina, who eloped with a farm labourer and ran away so many years ago, has been on my mind. I know my father, your grandfather and father-in-law abandoned her and forbade me to try to contact her, but now I have started praying for her. I believe she had twins and maybe other children. Please pray that one day there will be forgiveness and reconciliation between us all.

Ernest read the letter well and then he handed it back to his mother as the last part was just for her.

Libby-Ann asked the meaning of 'reconciliation', and her mother explained that it meant being friends together again.

"I would like that," she said. "It would be nice to have another aunt and uncle and cousins."

"Then each night we will all pray that it will happen," answered her mother.

Elspeth couldn't really remember her father very well, but their mother showed them all the photo of his face which she kept in a large gold locket that she wore around her neck.

"One day you will see him again," she said with a sigh. "You will just love your dear Papa so much!"

Chapter Two

The children were so happy that the holidays had arrived. Libby-Ann's governess also went on holiday, so there were no lessons. One morning at breakfast, which the children had together in the day nursery, their mother appeared.

"I think we should do as Papa suggested and all go to visit the Zoological Gardens in Regent's Park, London," she announced. "I have asked Cook to make us a picnic lunch basket, and Brownie will help us. He will drive us to Addiscombe Road Station, and then we will go by train to London. Polly!" she said to the nursery maid. "I will need you to come too, to help take care of Elspeth."

Polly was very excited. She had never before been to London or even on a train! "Please put on your sailor suits, and you must wear your hats. We will leave in an hour."

It was a lovely day for an outing. The sun was shining, but there was a nice breeze which stopped everyone from becoming too hot. Everyone was very excited about the outing, including their mama, who always loved adventures with her children. It made her feel happy to know that she was doing something which her husband had suggested. It was hard for all of them that he worked in such remote places and spent so little time at home.

At the station the two older children were given some money and told to buy their own return tickets to London. Mama wanted them to learn to be responsible, and she planned the following school year to allow Ernest to travel all the way home from St Pancras station by train, though Brownie would still accompany him.

Libby-Ann and Ernest were jumping up and down on the platform, interested in everything around them, while Mama and Polly sat on a bench with Elspeth until they heard the train steaming into the station. It stopped with a screech of brakes, and the family found an empty carriage where they could all sit together. Then the guard waved his green flag and the station master blew on his whistle, and slowly the train began to move with a clackety-clack noise as it gathered speed and went on its way to the next stop called Woodside. All the children wanted to sit near the window and see outside. In 1866 there was still a lot of countryside in the area south of central London, and the children looked out to see cows grazing in the fields which surrounded the more built up areas. Ernest had brought with him his notebook and pencil and wrote down all the train stations en route to London. The train belonged to the Mid-Kent Railway and passed through places like Elmers End and Beckenham on its way to the London terminus of Victoria station.

When they got off the train, their mother told them to keep very close to her because it was a busy part of London and they could easily get lost. Little Elspeth was struggling to keep up, and so Polly picked her up and carried her while Libby-Ann took the picnic basket which Polly had been carrying. Once they were out of the station precinct, they were able to catch a horse-drawn bus to take them to Regent's Park and the zoo. In those days the place was always called the Zoological Gardens, but many years later this was shortened to London Zoo.

Once they had reached the bus stop and all scrambled off, everyone was feeling quite tired and thirsty, so their mother suggested that they stop in the park and have a drink of the lovely homemade lemonade which cook had made for them. They sat on a bench and looked at all the ducks on the lake, but Libby-Ann and Ernest asked if they could explore.

"Just for a little while," answered their mother, "but once you have stretched your legs then come back, for we have lots to do and so many animals to see."

Ernest wished he had brought a ball, but even without one he and his sister had a great game of tag. It was such a lovely park that they could have happily played there all day! Then they went along to see the Regent's Park canal which flowed through the park and looked at the canal boats, admiring the painted roses on the outside of many of them. Soon they heard their mother calling them. It was now time for them to go and pay their money to get into the zoo, which they did and then entered through the turnstile gates.

"Please, Mama?" asked Libby-Ann. "Please can we go to see Jumbo first?"

"I think that is an excellent idea," answered her mother, and they found directions to the elephant house.

Jumbo was a very famous elephant who had been captured in East Africa in 1862. After a few adventures, he was bought by London Zoo in 1865. He was still quite a small elephant then, but his keeper named him 'Jumbo' and the name stuck. He soon began to grow and was one of the largest elephants ever known in captivity. He lived for almost seventeen years at the zoo before being sold to an American circus. Jumbo was a great favourite with Queen Victoria and her children. A saddle which was called a 'howdah' was made for him, and he was trained to give children rides. The rides cost a penny— which was a lot of money in Victorian times.

Jumbo loved to be outdoors, so when he was locked in his house sometimes he banged himself against the doors, trying to get outside. This damaged his lovely big tusks.

When Ernest, Libby-Ann and Elspeth visited the zoo, Jumbo had not been fully trained to give rides, but he was happily wandering around his compound, and when he saw the children looking at him he came lumbering over and pushed his long trunk through the fencing.

"I think he wants something to eat," exclaimed Libby-Ann to her mother.

"Let's see what he might like. I have heard that he likes sugar lumps, so I brought some with me," she said to the children. "Do you want to give him one, Ernest?" she asked her son.

Ernest was a bit scared, but he wasn't going to let his little sisters know, so he boldly answered, "Yes please, Mama." His mother put a lump onto his hand, and very gingerly Ernest put it near Jumbo's trunk. With a huge sucking noise the elephant took it, swung his trunk into the air and then into his mouth, eating the sugar lump with great relish!

"Can I have a go, Mama?" asked Libby-Ann. Her mother nodded and put a sugar lump in her hand.

She stretched out her hand and let Jumbo take it but started to giggle uncontrollably because it felt so funny when the elephant took it from her.

"Me too!" cried Elspeth.

"I think you are too small, dear," explained her mother, "but Polly can do it for you."

"Can I really?" asked Polly, her eyes growing large at the thought. She was terrified and had never in her whole life thought she would see a live elephant, let alone give one a sugar lump!

"It's easy!" said Libby-Ann. "Ernest and I dare you to do it for Elspeth!"

Very slowly, Polly put out her hand with the sugar lump, shaking so much that she almost dropped it.

When Jumbo had taken it, everyone clapped and Polly went bright pink with the excitement of it all.

"I think that's enough for now," said a deep voice. The children looked around and saw the keeper coming out of the elephant house. "Too much sugar will make him agitated, and he has to have his lesson soon."

"What lesson?" asked Libby-Ann. "Does he go to elephant school?"

"No, miss," replied the keeper, "but he is learning to walk carefully along some of the paths around the Zoological Gardens wearing a saddle. Soon he will begin to give rides to children, but he has to be taught to do it safely and properly. He's a good boy, though, and a quick learner. Elephants are very intelligent creatures, and once they have learnt something they never forget it."

"I wish I could remember all my governess teaches me and never forget it!" said Libby-Ann with a sigh.

"Me too," added Ernest. "I just can't remember all the Latin and French words we have to learn at school. The masters keep a birch cane in the corner and sometimes beat us if we get them wrong."

"Do you eat up all your dinners?" asked the keeper. "This young elephant has quite an appetite. He consumes 91kg of hay, a barrel of potatoes, 2 bushels of oats, 15 loaves of bread and lots and lots of onions every single day as well as drinking buckets of water!"

"My goodness!" exclaimed their mother. "I'm glad that you lot don't eat that much—we would all be in the poor house! However, talking about food has made me feel hungry. Shall we find somewhere and eat our picnic?"

The family said goodbye to the keeper and Jumbo and promised to come back and have a ride when he started giving them.

After eating the lovely picnic lunch which Cook had made for them and finishing her delicious homemade lemonade, their mother made them all sit and rest for a little while. Elspeth was very tired and fell asleep sat on Polly's lap. Ernest and Libby-Ann played 'I spy with my little eye' with their mother until their sister woke up again. Sitting on a bench in the zoo, there was a lot to see, so it made the game great fun.

"Where shall we go next?" asked their mother.

"I want to go to the insect house," Ernest replied at once.

"Alright," agreed Mama, and they made their way there. Libby-Ann was interested in the butterflies and moths because of the work which her father did but was not at all keen on seeing the spiders and other creepy-crawly creatures. After a while she became a bit bored and wandered off from the rest of the group, forgetting that her mother had told them all to stay together. She found a sort of tank where many beetles were living, and she thought how ugly the big black ones looked. They seemed to have claws which wanted to grab her and she felt scared, so she ran out of the insect house into the bright sunshine.

Chapter Three

"That's better," she said to herself, and as she looked around she saw a lake where the penguins were living. It had railings around it, and quite a lot of people were standing in front of it, making it hard for her to see the animals. Libby-Ann wasn't very tall for her age, but being determined to see, she kept pushing and slipping between the grown-ups until she was right at the front. How cute the penguins were as they waddled around or dived and swam in the pool! One waddled very near her, and Libby-Ann managed to put her arm through the railings, even though they were very close together, but she hadn't bothered to read the notice which warned her not to do so! One beautiful King Penguin waddled up to her. She was mesmerized by his gorgeous colouring and reached out to touch him. He thought she had a fish to give him and snapped at her fingers. What a great yell Libby-Ann gave! It made a keeper come running and scared away all the penguins near her. When she tried to bring out her arm, she couldn't move it. It was well and truly stuck! Now she screamed even louder, and everyone around her tried to help.

"Where are your parents?" asked the keeper, then getting no reply from the sobbing child, he looked at the crowd which had gathered and told everyone to go away except the parents of the child. The keeper looked very flustered and as if he really didn't know what to do next. He was obviously happier throwing fish to his beloved penguins than he was coping with a sobbing child who had her arm stuck in the railings! Most people moved away when asked, but a very kind young lady came and bent down near Libby-Ann and began to talk quietly to her.

"You do seem to be in a bit of a mess," she said in her quiet, sing-song sort of voice. At once Libby-Ann felt a bit better and stopped screaming.

"What is your name, dear, and where is your mama?" she asked gently, picking up Libby-Ann's sailor hat which had dropped on the path with all the struggles to free her arm.

"I'm Elizabeth-Ann Mountjoy Evans," answered Libby-Ann, "and my mama and brother, sister and nursemaid are all inside the insect house."

"That's good, dear," the lady said. "Why don't I send my friend to go and find them while we try to get your arm free?"

The kind young lady, who told Libby-Ann she was called Hattie, motioned to a young man who was standing nearby.

"Can you go to the insect house and try to find Mrs Mountjoy Evans to come to help her daughter?"

The young man smiled and nodded and ran in the direction of the insect house.

Hattie tried very gently to release Libby-Ann's arm, but by now it was beginning to swell, and so she realised it would be almost impossible to get it out. She looked at the keeper and told him to find someone from the maintenance department to come with a saw. Libby-Ann heard the word 'saw' and shrieked in terror once more.

"Are they going to saw my arm off?" she asked Hattie.

Hattie tried to calm her down.

"No, sweetie, they may need to saw the railings—not you!" she said. Libby-Ann was very relieved to hear that!

Back in the insect house, nobody had noticed that Libby-Ann was missing. There were so many exhibits, and Mrs Mountjoy Evans and Ernest were totally captivated by the butterfly section where they were looking at the beautiful butterflies from many places around the world, including the Congo. Ernest was so enjoying being home from boarding school and having his mother to himself for a few minutes that he didn't think about his sister. She would be looking at some other interesting specimens, he was sure.

After a short while, Polly came up to her mistress with little Elspeth by her side.

"Excuse me, madam," she said politely, "may I take Elspeth out in the sunshine to see the giraffes and other big animals? She's a bit bored in here."

"Of course! That's a good idea," answered Mama. "I'll bring the others over and meet you by the giraffe when we have finished here."

Polly and Elspeth went happily outside, and Ernest and his mother continued to talk about butterflies. When they thought about it afterwards, they did recall in the background the noise of a child screaming, but it was distant and they had no idea it was Libby-Ann. It wasn't until they were almost ready to leave that Ernest began to look around for his sister and a young man entered the insect house calling out in a very loud voice for Mrs Mountjoy Evans.

In alarm the children's mother identified herself to the young man, who told her about Libby-Ann's accident. Ernest held his mother's hand very tightly as she went as white as a sheet, and together they ran out of the insect house and down to the penguins' enclosure.

In spite of all the keeper had tried to do, once again there was a crowd gathering around Libby-Ann and Hattie. The young man began to order them all away, and everyone was relieved when they saw a couple of men with a cart full of tools rushing down the path to help.

When the keeper appeared, all the penguins came near, for they were hungry and it was past feeding time. Ernest was almost in tears when he saw his sister's arm, now looking very swollen and a bit of a strange bluish colour. Once again the sweet young lady, Hattie, took command.

"Keeper, why don't you take Libby-Ann's brother and let him help you feed these hungry animals?" she suggested. "That would be the best thing while these men try to remove the railings."

The keeper nodded and took Ernest with him to the other side of the pool, where most of the crowd followed them as they wanted to see the penguins being fed.

"Thank you so much," said Mama, now feeling calmer after the first shock had worn off. "I don't know how this happened, but I am so grateful to you."

The workmen were very efficient and quickly removed the two railings on each side of Libby-Ann's arm. Her mother gathered her up into her arms and began to cry with relief. It was good that the penguins were eating, because none tried to come and escape before the workmen made the barrier safe again.

"I'm so sorry, Mama. I didn't mean to be naughty," said Libby-Ann, starting to sob again.

"Darling, we won't talk about that now," said her mother, "but I think we do need to get you to a hospital and make sure that your arm is going to be alright. It looks very swollen to me."

"I am a probationer nurse," said Hattie. "I am in the Nightingale School of Nursing at St. Thomas' hospital. I know it is over the river, but I am sure that you would get help there."

As they were talking about this, a very important-looking gentleman came striding over.

"I hear this young lady has had a bit of trouble," he said. "I am Alexander Trope, the governor of these Zoological Gardens. I am very sorry. I understand your arm became caught in the railings. Did you not see the notice which told people not to put their hands through?"

"No, sir, there were lots of people, and I just edged my way to the front so that I could see the penguins, and one came near to me, so I thought I could stroke it. I didn't see any notice. I'm very sorry for all the trouble I have caused," replied Libby-Ann. With this she began to find the tears pouring out of her eyes again.

"Now, my dear," said Mr Trope, "I didn't mean to tell you off or make you cry. I simply needed to know what happened for me to make a report and see that such a thing never happens again."

"I'm Mrs Mountjoy Evans," said the children's mother. "I wasn't with Elizabeth-Ann when this happened. I hadn't realized that she had left the insect house—so I am as much to blame as she is."

"It's really not about blaming anyone, madam," he replied, "but I do need to be able to keep all my visitors safe. Now your name is very interesting. Are you by chance related to Mr Ernest Mountjoy Evans? He is one of the best butterfly hunters I have known. At present he is in the jungles of the Congo chasing butterflies."

"Why, he is my husband!" said Mama in surprise. "That is why Ernest junior and I were so long in the insect house looking at specimens from the Congo, and I guess Libby-Ann became a little tired of waiting for us and came out to see the penguins. Oh dear, my youngest is with her nursery maid looking at the giraffe. I need to tell her where we are and what has happened!"

Just then Ernest and the keeper arrived, having fed the penguins, so he was quickly dispatched to find Polly and Elspeth.

"I think that Libby-Ann should get to a hospital and have her arm treated; it is very swollen," Hattie reminded everyone.

"Of course! Forgive me, my dear, for not dealing with that at once. If you would all come with me to my office, I will arrange transport at once."

"Does that mean we cannot see any more animals?" asked Ernest. "I had hoped to see lions and tigers and lots of other things today!"

Mr Trope smiled. "Well, that is one thing I can do for you all," he said happily. "Your visit today has clearly been spoilt. I can give you all tickets to come back another time. In fact," he said very thoughtfully, "I should be able to arrange a season ticket for you seeing that your papa is catching butterflies for us!"

"Oh, thank you, sir," replied Ernest and his mother, and Libby-Ann nodded her head in thanks too.

Very soon a horse-drawn cab arrived to take everyone to the hospital. Mr Trope suggested that it would be far quicker to attend the University College Hospital, which the North London Hospital had recently been renamed.

"You see, madam," he said, "not only is it nearer, but they also have a surgeon there with a great expertise in putting a patient to sleep with ether while they do operations."

Hattie was agreeable to that, and so she and her young man said goodbye to the family, though she was disappointed not to have taken them to St. Thomas' Hospital where Florence Nightingale had set up her nursing school so recently in order to give nurses proper training and recognition.

By the time they arrived at the hospital, Elspeth had fallen asleep on Polly's knee, and Libby-Ann was almost asleep herself. She felt very tired, and it was only the pain in her arm which kept her awake.

She was a bit worried, too, when she heard Mr Trope talk about operations! Surely, the doctors wouldn't have to cut her open! Would she have to stay in the hospital all alone until she was better? There were no places for parents to stay with their children such as there are in hospitals these days.

When they arrived at the hospital, the cabby told them that he would wait to see if he was needed. Mr Trope was taking care of all the bills, and he had given the children's mother a letter to vouch for this.

Mrs Mountjoy Evans took Libby-Ann into the hospital to register and present the letter about payment, for in Victorian times medical help was not free. She and Mama were directed into a cubicle where Libby-Ann was put onto a bed. It seemed very big and high up compared with her little bed in the night nursery at home. Everyone else stayed in the waiting room out of the way, but there were no toys to play with or comics to read. It was hot, stuffy and very boring!

After a while a doctor came to see Libby-Ann. He read the letter and then asked all about the incident before examining her arm. By now the arm was looking a beautiful shade of purple and was still swollen. The doctor gently felt up and down her arm and asked where it hurt the most. Then Libby-Ann had to raise it and turn it, and because she managed to do this without too much trouble, the doctor decided that the bones had not been broken. At this time x-ray machines had not been invented, so they were not able to look at her bones in this way.

Libby-Ann was so relieved! It didn't seem that anyone would cut her arm open after all!

The doctor finished writing his notes and then went to find a nurse. He asked the her to bandage the arm, though not too tightly because of all the swelling, and finally to put it into a sling.

"I suggest that you keep the sling on for a week. If you have a lot more pain or any other worries, then please go and see your own family doctor. I think that after a week you will be able to do everything much as usual—but take care that you don't put your arm through railings or stroke penguins again!" he said with a chuckle.

So, looking very impressive with her arm in a sling, Libby-Ann was able to join the rest of the family. They all piled back into the taxi cab, and their mother asked to be taken to Victoria station, for after all the excitement of the day it was definitely time to catch the train home. Ernest sat in the front by the cabby and enjoyed seeing some of the sights of London as they drove back. The cabby was a cockney and kept talking to Ernest in the cockney rhyming slang and sometimes saying words backwards, so the boy didn't really understand very much of the conversation, but it was fun even so.

On the train going home, they had a whole compartment to themselves. There was so much to talk about! It had been a very exciting day, even though they'd had a few more adventures than anyone had planned! The family were also on a later train than they had expected and so thought that Brownie would not be there to meet them, meaning they might have to walk a mile or so uphill to their home.

However, when they alighted from the train and went outside

the station, there was dear Brownie with the carriage. How good it was to see him, for they were feeling tired and Elspeth was asleep in Polly's arms, while Libby-Ann's arm was throbbing.

It didn't take long to drive home, where Cook was waiting for them. Wonderful food smells were coming from the kitchen, and Ernest spoke for all of them when he announced that he was starving!

Of course, Cook and Brownie had to hear about Jumbo, the insect house and Libby-Ann's accident in the penguin enclosure and all that followed.

Chapter Four

That night, Libby-Ann woke up because her arm hurt so much. The children slept in the attic at the top of the house in what was called the 'night nursery'. Polly slept in a room with Elspeth, but the two other children had their own rooms.

Somehow, everything always seems much worse in the middle of the night when it is dark and lonely. There was a gaslight, but Libby-Ann wasn't allowed to light that by herself, and Polly had taken away the candle once she was in bed in case she lit it and the bedclothes caught fire. Libby-Ann had always been the child who had accidents! Now she had managed to get herself into trouble again! Although her mother hadn't scolded her in public at the zoo, she could tell that she wasn't too pleased at the day being spoilt by her naughtiness at leaving the insect house on her own. Libby-Ann hadn't meant to be naughty, but she was what her mother called 'very impulsive' and did things without thinking about what might happen.

That night, she felt very sorry for herself. Big tears trickled down her cheeks, and she tried to wipe them away with her one good hand, but it didn't work very well. She knew she had been quite brave when it all happened, but now she no longer felt brave and she realised that she should never have left the insect house without asking Mama.

However, she thought to herself, Mama was busy with Ernest as she so often was when he was home. She was sure that her Mama liked Ernest much more than herself. He was the eldest and also a boy. He would carry on the important family name of Mountjoy Evans when he grew up. She was only a girl, and everyone knew that girls weren't so important. Ernest could be an explorer or something else very exciting when he was older, whereas she would have to learn to sew and manage a house and do boring things like sit at tea parties and talk to people and raise money for the poor!

By now Libby-Ann was really sobbing. She thought perhaps Polly would come and comfort her, but Polly adored Elspeth and did very little for her or Ernest. Not that Ernest would want a nursemaid helping him! He had grown up so much since he started at boarding school. If only she could attend a school, maybe she would have a special friend, someone who really liked her! Once, when her father was at home, she had asked him if she could attend a local school, but he had told her she was too young and that he wanted her to stay at home with a governess.

In fact, Libby-Ann did like her governess, Miss Austerberry. She was kind and patient, even though her pupil didn't enjoy many of the lessons and was hopeless at making her sampler. She thought that she would be sewing it right up until the time she was grown up. Libby-Ann seemed to spend more time taking out stitches where she had made mistakes than she did putting in new ones! There were lots of stains where she had pricked her finger and marked the canvas. Her Papa just laughed when he saw it and remarked that she would never make a needlewoman!

Thinking about her governess reminded Libby-Ann that she had made a promise to her, that all through the holidays she would say her prayers at bedtime. Last night she had forgotten completely. She wished that prayers were more interesting. Reciting old-fashioned prayers and collects didn't seem to mean very much, although she always remembered to ask God to bless her papa wherever he might be and keep him safe as well as all the members of their household, including Rex their spaniel and Rafiki their parrot.

Gradually, Libby-Ann stopped crying and started to say her prayers. When she got to the last bit, which was 'God bless me', she thought she would add a few words of her own, so said, "I'm sorry I'm so impulsive and naughty. Please make me good and please let people love me too, like they do Ernest and Elspeth, if that's not too hard for you. Amen."

Then something which seemed very strange happened to Libby-Ann. It was as if someone wrapped her up in a soft blanket and cuddled her to sleep. The pain left her arm, and soon she was dreaming of elephants and butterflies and penguins waddling around!

The next day, Polly came to wake her and to help her wash and dress and was very gentle with her arm. It really did look a horrible colour! The children had breakfast together in the day nursery, and then Ernest discussed what they should do to amuse themselves. Elspeth was so much younger that she had her own routine and still played 'baby' games. Usually, Libby-Ann was such a tomboy that she and Ernest spent as much of the holidays out of doors as they could.

He had taught her to play cricket, which she loved, and they also loved climbing trees as well as trying to catch butterflies.

They were just talking about what to do when their mother came up. She was up early! Normally, Mama had her breakfast in bed and then got up and prepared to go visiting or receive visitors.

"I've come to join you for breakfast," she said cheerfully. "I want to make sure that you are managing Libby-Ann. How is that arm feeling today?"

She looked at her daughter and saw the dark rings around her eyes and thought that she could not have slept very well. She had intended to scold Libby-Ann for running off, but one look at her made her think that she had been punished enough by the pain she was suffering, so she decided not to say anything more.

"It does hurt quite a lot, Mama," answered Libby-Ann, "but not as much as it did in the night. We were just wondering what we could do today. It's such a nice day, I really would like to go outside, but I can't play cricket or climb trees with Ernest."

After thinking for a few minutes, their mother had an idea.

"Would you like to go for a walk and see the windmill? Brownie can go with you because I want him to enquire about milling some corn in a few days. Mr Alwen, the miller, might show you round the windmill if he's not too busy. Anyway, it's a nice walk and not too far. Just promise me that you will all keep together!" said Mama.

"We promise," Ernest and Libby-Ann said together as Libby-Ann blushed a little as she remembered what had happened the day before.

"Can I go too?" asked Elspeth.

"No, darling," answered Mama. "You will stay with Polly. Maybe she will help you wash your dolly's clothes. You are too small to go everywhere with the big children."

Elspeth seemed to like the idea of washing the doll's clothes, so she smiled happily at Polly.

An hour later, the children began their walk to the Shirley windmill. Shirley was not really too far from the Upper Addiscombe Road where they lived. They walked one on each side of Brownie and chatted happily to him. He and Cook were so much part of the family that they didn't really seem like servants but more like family friends. Every now and then a carriage would pass them, and the children tried to peek inside to see if they knew who was sitting there. Often Brownie knew the groom or the footman. In fact, the family shared some stables for their horse and carriage, so he could sometimes recognise the horses as well as the people. Once they had left Addiscombe and walked up the Shirley Road, which, as Ernest aptly said, should really be called a hill because it was quite steep, they were able to walk through fields to the mill.

As always, the children were looking for butterflies. August was a good month to see them, and on sunny days they sat on the wild flowers sucking nectar.

"Look!" said Ernest. "There is a lovely Red Admiral." The butterfly stayed still for several seconds, and Libby-Ann was able to admire it. Then she saw a Meadow Blue, which was one of her favourites because blue was her favourite colour. In fact, not only did she have blue eyes, but that morning Polly had tied her ringlets with a blue hair ribbon. Normally Ernest would have raced his sister to the windmill, but he could see that her arm hurt even though it was in a sling, so he walked by her side.

The windmill was big, and they could see it from quite a distance. In fact, the mill was a landmark on the hill. Mr Alwen the miller had been working in the mill ever since he was a boy.

As they approached the mill, they saw Mr Alwen standing outside enjoying the sunshine. He waved as he saw Brownie and the children.

"Good morning," he said politely, lifting his flat cap to Libby-Ann, which she thought was very gallant of him. "What can I do for you young people?"

Brownie spoke. "I have an enquiry about bringing some corn from Mrs Mountjoy Evans for you to grind into flour. She would like it done in a few days' time. Do you have time to do it?"

"Come inside," said Mr Alwen, and the children needed no further invitation and rushed into the windmill. It was noisy and dusty inside. The machinery was working, and the miller's assistant was tying up a sack of flour.

While the miller was talking with Brownie and fixing a date, the children began to look around the ground floor. It was so interesting. There were several bags of corn waiting to be ground. One of them was open, and Ernest put his hand in it and allowed the corn to run through his fingers. As he did this, something glinted in the sack. He put his hand in and saw that there was a gold sovereign among the corn. "Wow! What was that doing there?" he thought to himself. "It must have fallen in when the sack was being filled! I can't leave it there to get ground up between the big mill stones!" Quickly, he picked up the coin and slipped it into his pocket.

Ernest was sure that no one else had seen him remove the coin, and he thought to himself, "Finders, keepers. This makes me really rich! I can buy all sorts of sweets from the school tuck shop next term! Everyone will want to be my friend, and even the big boys won't bully me if I treat them!"

Libby-Ann had been looking at a little mouse which she had seen darting across the stone floor. She wondered if she should tell the miller because it would eat the corn but decided that there must be many mice in the mill, and she didn't want this little creature to be killed. It looks so sweet with its whiskers and pink nose!

"Children," called the miller, "would you like to see the rest of the mill?"

"Oh yes, please!" they both answered.

"Let me tell you about this windmill. It is called a post mill, and my father built it long ago. I inherited it when he died and all was well for a while. Then there was a fire—and with so much dry dust around, the fire quickly spread so that most of the mill was burnt down. It was terrible! It happened so quickly, and there was little we could do to stop it. I remember the next day coming and looking at it. All my father's hard work and my livelihood lay in ashes! At first I didn't know what to do, and I felt like crying in despair. Then I said to myself, "John, your father would be ashamed of you. There is just one thing to do. You have enough gold sovereigns saved up to rebuild and start again!"

Hearing the words 'gold sovereigns' made Ernest feel uncomfortable, and he flushed a little as he put his hand into his pocket and felt the treasure he had found.

"Anyway," continued Mr Alwen, "I managed to do that. It was like starting all over again, but I rebuilt the mill to be even stronger than the first one. There are five storeys, and you will have to be careful going up the narrow stairs. Can you manage them, my dear?" he asked Libby-Ann kindly.

"I'll help her," answered Brownie. "Elizabeth-Ann won't want to miss this adventure, I know."

On their conducted tour, which did take a long time as Libby-Ann found it quite hard to climb, they went right up to the sails. The tower was 55 feet high (16.76 metres).

They saw the miller's assistant haul up bags of corn through a hatch, and then the corn was ground by being crushed through huge millstones. Although it was hot and dusty inside the windmill, it was very interesting.

"What a lot of work to make flour for bread!" Libby-Ann exclaimed. "I shall appreciate my bread even more now!"

When they had climbed down the stairs, mostly going backwards because it was so narrow and steep, they went outside again into the bright sunlight.

"This mill is 21 feet (6.40 metres) around the base," explained Mr Alwen. "It is very solid and should last for many, many years to come."

"I hope so," said Ernest. "Thank you so much for showing us around." He wanted to go home again as soon as possible and hide his treasure away. It felt as if it was burning a hole in his pocket! He didn't want anyone at home to know about his gold sovereign—he had found it and it was his! He would keep it and take it to school!

The children waved goodbye to the miller and walked back with Brownie, who noticed that Ernest was rather subdued. Normally the boy chattered all the time and was looking for butterflies in every field.

"You all right, Master Ernest?" he enquired.

"Yes, of course!" answered Ernest almost rudely. "Why shouldn't I be?"

"No reason at all, young sir. I just thought that you were walking slowly," Brownie answered.

"Libby-Ann can't chase butterflies today with her arm in a sling, so I'll just walk with you," replied Ernest. Somehow Brownie thought something was wrong, but he kept the thoughts to himself.

By the time they arrived home, Cook had lunch ready and they were all hungry and thirsty. Once they had eaten, Ernest ran to his room and tied up his treasure in a clean handkerchief and put it in the bottom of his school trunk with a Latin textbook on top. He was sure it would be safe there! He should have been really happy and excited, but somehow it wasn't like that. In his mind, he kept having thoughts that he had stolen that money. Really, it must have fallen out of someone's pocket and into the sack. Then he had other thoughts that told him nobody would know whose sack it was and nobody would know that he had taken it. Some of the boys at school picked up things and always declared that the finders were keepers! It must be alright. However, he began to feel more and more miserable.

To try and forget the thoughts, Ernest decided to climb the apple tree and take with him his favourite book to read. Libby-Ann had been told to lie down and rest as she looked so tired, and for once, she didn't mind because she had slept so little the night before.

Even the book didn't stop the bad thoughts, and Ernest became even more miserable and grumpy. Rex had followed him out to the apple tree, and when he barked for attention Ernest shouted at him and even threw down his book, hitting the very surprised dog on his leg. Rex gave a yelp of pain. At once Ernest felt very sorry, for he loved the dog and had never hurt him before. He climbed down from the tree and hugged the dog and said he was sorry. What was the matter with him? He began to wish that he had never found the shiny gold sovereign.

Chapter Five

Far away in the middle of Africa, exploring the area of the Virunga volcanic mountains, Dr Ernest Mountjoy Evans was pleased because it had been a good day. He had been very excited when he had spotted a large and beautiful butterfly which he thought might be a new species. He managed to catch it in his net and was able to make a detailed drawing of the specimen before the light began to fade. Their native cook had made a good meal for the exploration team, and afterwards they had retired to the tent for the night. Two other men shared his tent and had become his close friends. Each night they got out their Bibles and read, discussed and prayed together.

Only a week previously, Ernest had realised that he wasn't a Christian but was as heathen as the pygmies who lived in the forest around him. He had always thought he was a Christian because he had been baptised into the Christian faith when he was an infant and then had been confirmed when at boarding school along with all the other boys in his class when he was thirteen. Through reading the Bible with his tentmates, he had come to understand that being a Christian was all about having a relationship with Jesus and that Jesus had really lived on earth and had died to take the punishment for all his misdeeds. It had been a real revelation to him, and with the help of his friends he asked Jesus to be his Saviour and Friend.

What a wonderful week it had been! Ernest now found the Bible came alive when he read it, and when he prayed it was not just reciting but talking to his new friend, Jesus. He also found that he was longing to go home to his family and tell them about Jesus and help them to understand too.

That evening, the three friends prayed together for their families and thanked God for all his blessings to them, then blew out the paraffin lamp and settled to sleep.

They had become accustomed to all the jungle noises at night, mostly made by insects in the mountains, and so quickly fell asleep.

About three in the morning, there were strange noises, and all of the men woke up. What was happening? Peering out through their tent into the moonlight, they saw a scene of chaos! A whole group of pygmies dressed in headdresses and carrying spears, bows and arrows surrounded their camp. The three friends withdrew into the tent and looked at each other.

"It seems we are being attacked," whispered Richard. "What shall we do?"

"Pray!" was David's instant response.

"Father, we don't know what is happening, but we put ourselves in your hands. Amen," he said and Richard and Ernest quietly whispered 'Amen' too.

Their knapsacks were by their beds, and these contained their notebooks and specimens.

"Let's put them on our backs," suggested Ernest. "If we are captured, we may be able to save them."

The three friends did this, and a moment or so later their tent was slashed open by a machete and they were grabbed by several small men, who tied their wrists together with jungle twine. The rest of the explorers were already tied, but the cook and native porters had fled into the forest.

The attackers started a fire and burnt the campsite down. All the men could do was watch helplessly as they saw everything destroyed. All the things they needed to survive on this expedition had gone up in flames!

Each man was grabbed by two pygmies and led through the thick forest. The natives might be small men, but they were very strong and there was no getting away from them! As they walked into the forest, they seemed to be climbing because it became more difficult to breathe and the vegetation changed from broad-leafed trees to bamboo. It was moonlight, which did help the men to see the trail, but suddenly two of their number fell into a net set to trap animals. In the confusion which followed, another explorer tried to break free from his captors. The pygmy warriors immediately shot a poisoned arrow at him, and he fell to the ground. It was a warning to them all! Now only Richard, David and Ernest were left standing.

Their captors made them to keep walking, and eventually the three men came to a clearing where they saw a small village with very poor mud huts. They were pushed into one of them and seemed to fall into a small pit. One of the pygmies stood guard over them with his bow and arrow at the ready. They knew if they tried to escape, then he would not hesitate to shoot a poisoned arrow at them.

They had fallen onto the floor, and it was dirty and smelly.

"Let's pray together," suggested Richard. And so the three men thanked God that they were still alive and asked him to help them and keep them safe.

"We don't understand what this is about, Father," Richard prayed, "but please help us to love and help these pygmies, and take care of our families if we are to die."

Finally the three men dozed off into a fitful sleep, not knowing what the next day would bring. Ernest thought of his lovely family at home and silently asked God that they would come to know him in a real way just as he had done. "Whatever happens to me, I know that my life is in God's hands. I am a forgiven man, and should I die (which seems very likely), I know I will go to heaven," he said to himself.

When they woke the next morning, as the sun rose almost exactly at six in the morning (as it does on the equator), they were stiff and cold. In the mountains it can be very cold at night, and they were only wearing pyjamas. In fact, they couldn't help laughing at each other because they looked so funny in pyjamas and knapsacks!

Only these three men had survived the raid upon the explorers' camp. They had no idea what their fate would be. It was almost impossible for a white man to survive without good food and water which had been boiled and purified. They had just a few possessions in their knapsacks, but even those could be stolen from them. All their Congolese staff had deserted them, and even if they went to the authorities and reported the raid, it would take weeks for them to trek to the nearest settlement, let alone bring a rescue party out to search for them. How could they survive?

Chapter Six

"I've been thinking," announced Mama the day after the trip to the windmill. "I have just re-read your Papa's letter, and he has asked us to start reading the Bible and praying together. I know we always attend church, but I think as well as that we should do more. I thought that you two older children could have dinner with me every evening through the holidays instead of eating in the nursery, and afterwards we could try to read some of the Bible as Papa suggested. What do you think?"

"Me too?" asked Elspeth, never wanting to be left out.

"No, darling, you are too small. You will still have your dinner in the nursery with Polly, but maybe afterwards I could come up and tell you a Bible story before you go to bed?"

"Yes please, Mama," Elspeth answered, thinking how nice it would be to have her Mama tell her stories. Polly couldn't read very well, and most of her stories were read to her by Libby-Ann.

"Can we really have dinner downstairs with you?" asked Ernest, thinking the Bible reading bit might be boring but that the dinner would be fabulous!

"Every evening, except if I am invited out to dinner or other people are invited here. That doesn't often happen when your Papa is away. I will enjoy your company. Polly!" Mama continued, looking at the nursery maid. "You will make sure that clean best clothes are ready for the children every evening, and they must bathe and dress for dinner at six."

"Yes, ma'am," answered Polly, with a little curtsey.

"I have been thinking about something else too," Mama continued. "We should go away for a holiday while Ernest is home from school. I thought we should go to the seaside. What do you think of that idea?"

"OOOOh yes!" Libby-Ann said in excitement. "That would be lovely!" The other children agreed.

"Where will we go?" asked Ernest, who was already thinking about all the adventures they could have.

"I was thinking about Dorset. I will try to rent a cottage in a village near Weymouth. It will be near your Grandmama and Grandpapa, and it is a long time since you have seen them. We will visit them, but as they are no longer used to having noisy children around, we will not stay with them. I will begin to make enquiries today so that we can go later next week, so long as the doctor is pleased with Libby-Ann's arm and she can take the sling and bandages off."

All this was very exciting news for the children. Secretly, Ernest was very glad that they would not be staying at his grandparents' house. He was a bit afraid of his mother's parents, who were very strict and definitely approved of the Victorian idea that 'children should be seen and not heard'. He knew they always grumbled that Libby-Ann was a tomboy and should learn to be a young lady and use her proper name of Elizabeth-Ann. It would be much more fun in a cottage on their own!

That evening, Ernest and Libby-Ann felt grown up as they dressed in their best clothes and went to the dining room for dinner! Brownie waited on them, and they had soup, main dinner and dessert! Mama had decided not to have cheese afterwards in case it gave the children bad dreams, so once the dishes had been cleared away she found the very large family Bible in which was written all the important family events like births, deaths and marriages and brought it to the table.

"I have decided not to start at the very beginning but to read about Jesus, so we will begin with the gospels," she told them and opened the book at St Matthew.

It started with a long list of names, which did seem pretty boring, but Mama explained that it was to tell people about the family tree of Jesus—who he was—because the person who had been promised as a Saviour for the Jews was to come from King David's family.

"There aren't many women mentioned," commented Libby-Ann, who was beginning to get interested as her mother explained things so well in her beautiful, gentle voice.

"Well, dear, in those days, even as today, the families took the name of the father. There are three women mentioned, and they are foreign women and one of them had a bad reputation. It's interesting, isn't it, that they were included in Jesus' family line. We would be shocked if we were introduced to such people, but God had accepted them. I read this bit of the gospel earlier so that I could understand it before we read it together and looked up who these women were. I think we shall have a lot to learn by reading this book together.

"Now we must pray for Papa and also remember his sister, Ernestina, and her family as he asked us to do."

Mrs Mountjoy Evans found it very difficult to lead the prayer time because she only knew how to recite prayers she had learnt by heart as a child. She just asked God to bless all those in the family including Ernestina, her own parents, sister and their family as well as their own household. Then they all said the Lord's Prayer together and a loud 'Amen'.

Ernest let out a sigh of relief when it was over. It wasn't as bad as he had expected, and the family tree bit had been quite interesting.

That night he couldn't sleep. The problem of the gold sovereign kept coming into his thoughts. He knew deep down he had stolen it. Maybe it belonged to someone really poor who needed it badly. Perhaps he should tell his mama what he had done.

The next day was Sunday, and after breakfast everyone was dressed in their best and ready to go in the carriage to morning church. The family had their own pew in the parish church, for which Father paid an annual rent. The children found church boring. The singing of the hymns and psalms and even the chants which were sung off and on throughout the service were not too bad, but they didn't understand the long words in the prayers and sermon. The vicar had such a monotonous voice, and he seemed to drone on and on. All the children were expected to behave like little adults, sitting very still and quiet in uncomfortable clothes. Normally Ernest just whiled away the time by thinking his own thoughts, mostly about butterflies and exploring strange lands. However, in the middle of the sermon he was brought back from his daydreams with a start. The vicar suddenly became excited and proclaimed in a loud voice that all sinners would go to hell unless they repented. Hell would be a horrible place, full of liars and thieves and those who were immoral. He urged his congregation to repent while there was still time. Who knew what the morrow might bring—today could be their last day on earth!

Ernest found his face going red as he thought about the gold sovereign he had hidden. His knees began to shake a little, and he found it hard to stand when the organ started and everyone got up to sing the hymn 'Onward, Christian Soldiers'.

When they arrived back at Myrtle House and everyone had climbed out of the carriage, Ernest asked his mother if he could speak to her on his own.

"This sounds very serious," said his mother with a smile, wondering whatever could be on Ernest's mind. "When you have had luncheon upstairs, come and find me. I will be in the library, so then we can have a chat."

After lunch Ernest made his way downstairs to the library, feeling very frightened. He wondered whatever his mama would think of him. He had let her down so badly, but he knew he would have no peace until he confessed what he had done. He gently tapped the library door.

"Come along in, dear," he heard his mother say. As he entered, she motioned to him to sit in a chair beside her. "Now, whatever is the matter? You look as white as a sheet. Are you feeling ill?"

"No, Mama, I'm quite well, thank you. But I do feel very bad. That is, bad about myself and very ashamed. I have done something very wicked. I think I will go to hell like the preacher said this morning."

Mama looked at her son and wondered whatever he could have done that made him think such a thing. He was not a lad who gave any trouble at all, and the staff had not complained about any bad behaviour.

"I think you had better confess and tell me the problem," Mama said to him very gently, seeing how upset Ernest was. He began to tell her the whole story of how he saw the glint of the gold, then he'd found the coin and then had slipped it into his pocket. It was all he could do not to cry, but now he was eleven and went to school, he must not be a baby and cry.

His mother listened and agreed that he had no right to take the gold sovereign. Finders were not keepers, and he must take it back to the mill and tell the story to the miller. Maybe he would know who had brought that sack of corn to him and be able to return the coin. Then they talked together about the importance of honesty even in the smallest things and how he needed to grow up to be a man who could be trusted.

"I am really sorry, Mama," said Ernest. "I knew it was wrong, but I kept having these other thoughts in my head. Please forgive me."

"You have let yourself down and to some extent let me down, but the ones from whom you must seek forgiveness are God and then the miller. You need to repent, as the vicar said this morning."

"What does 'repent' really mean?" asked Ernest.

"Get the dictionary from the shelf and look it up," suggested his Mother, so Ernest did as he was told.

"It says to feel sorry and regret and to feel such sorrow for sin as leads to amendment," read Ernest.

"Do you feel so sorry that you want to put things right?" asked Mama. "If you do, then I suggest that you go to your bedroom and tell God how sorry you are and that you want to give back the money and also to change your ways. Every Sunday the vicar reads a verse from the Bible that says 'If we confess our sins he (that is, God) is faithful and just to forgive us our sins and to cleanse us from all unrighteousness.' Do you understand this? When you have made things right with God, tomorrow Brownie will take you back and you can return the coin to Mr Alwen. I think doing that will be punishment enough. When you have done that I think you will feel altogether better."

Ernest did just as his mother had suggested. He went to his room and talked to God about the money and told him how sorry he was. Afterwards, he felt as if he was a stone lighter, he felt so happy, even though he still had to face the miller the next day.

Brownie took him back to the mill, while Libby-Ann went to see the doctor, who was very pleased at how well the arm had healed.

Mr Alwen was surprised to see Ernest looking so serious and asking if he could talk with him. He took him inside the mill, and although it was hard, Ernest told him what had happened and handed back the coin, asking forgiveness. Brownie waited outside and Ernest was glad, he was so ashamed of himself and didn't want all the servants to know how bad he had been.

"Thank you for being honest and bringing back the sovereign," said Mr Alwen. "Those sacks belonged to quite an elderly widow. I will go in person and return it to her. I'm sure she will be very grateful, and I'm sure you have learnt your lesson, son, and will never do such a thing again."

"No, sir, I will not," replied Ernest. "The days when I had it hidden were the most miserable of my whole life."

Once the coin had been returned, Ernest felt about six hundred times better! As they walked back through the field, he was running around looking for butterflies and was just his usual, happy self. Brownie hadn't known the details of what had happened but was so glad to see that the young master had sorted out his problems and was back to normal again.

Mother came up to the nursery at luncheon and could see at a glance that all was well. She was glad! It was hard to be a mother to three children with such a big responsibility, especially when their father was so far away and she could not ask his advice.

"Now I have great news for you," she told the children. "We will go on Friday to Dorset. We'll travel by train to London, then take another train to Weymouth. From there we will take a horse-drawn cab to a village called Abbotsbury and stay for two whole weeks! Polly, Cook and Brownie will come with us, and Constance will live in and take care of the house here as well as Rex and Rafiki while we are away. We will be very busy this week packing trunks, so I want you all to be extra good and helpful."

The children were very excited. A holiday at the seaside! They promised to be very good in the remaining days.

"Let's hope this sunshine stays and we can spend lots of time on the beach!" said Libby-Ann. "It will be such fun!"

Chapter Seven

Friday arrived, and everyone was up with the lark ready for the long train journey to Dorset. It was a drizzly sort of day, but that didn't dampen the children's spirits. They helped load the carriage, which had been hired to take them to the London terminus where they would catch the train. All the luggage was carefully stowed in the guard's van at the back of the train, and Brownie stayed there to look after it. He said he would enjoy talking to the guard about the railway.

It did take a very long time to arrive at Weymouth, but there were many interesting things to see along the way. Cook as usual had produced a fine picnic lunch for them all, after which the motion of the train caused all three children to doze and take a nap.

When they woke up, they were near the seaside, and from the carriage window they were able to gaze out at Poole Harbour. "It won't be long now," said their mother. At this news, the children were really pleased. They were a bit tired with being on the train. The sky had cleared, and by the time they arrived at Weymouth, the sun was shining again.

"The train stops here. Everyone please exit the train, taking all your baggage," shouted the guard.

Brownie had managed not only to get the trunks off the train but also engage a carriage to take them to Abbotsbury. It was several miles, but everywhere was new and interesting. First, they drove along the esplanade in Weymouth, admiring the sandy beach on one side and the impressive hotels on the other. Their mama told them about King George III who had come to stay in the town for the good of his health and made it into a popular resort. There were many bathing machines on the beach drawn by horses. These were huts on wheels where the visitors changed into their very elaborate bathing costumes, then the horses pulled them down into the shallow water where they were able to get out and bathe. Victorian people were extremely modest and even when swimming showed very little of their bodies. Men and women usually bathed in different areas of the beach, but they all enjoyed themselves immensely.

After leaving Weymouth town, the family proceeded up the Chickerell Road and into Chickerell village, then along the road to Portesham and finally, to Abbotsbury. The road was narrow, and most of the cottages along the way were small, thatched dwellings. It was very different from London and Croydon! Eventually they turned into a lane and drew up outside a thatched cottage. It looked lovely, with a pretty garden in front filled with summer flowers and a pink rose climbing around the front door; it was called 'Honeysuckle Cottage'. As they pulled up to a halt, a small, plump lady with very pink cheeks rushed over from a cottage on the other side of the road to greet them.

"Welcome!" she said. "I'm Mrs Bramley, and here is the key to the cottage. I live in Briar Cottage over the road, and I've put the kettle on and made some scones for your tea. If you would like to come in for a 'cuppa' after you have sorted yourselves out, I'd be honoured."

"That is very kind of you," Mama answered. "I'm sure the children and I would be delighted to do so while my staff unpack our belongings. We'll just choose our rooms and then come and have tea. Thank you very much."

They rushed inside to explore Honeysuckle Cottage. It had two nice sitting rooms in the front and a kitchen and a dining room at the rear. Upstairs there were two big bedrooms at the front, and then at the back of the house there were two more. Mama decided she would have one front room, and Polly, Elspeth and Libby-Ann would share the other. Ernest could choose which back room he wanted, leaving the other for Cook and Brownie. It would all be a bit of a squash compared with Myrtle House, but that would make it all the more fun.

"Let's go and have tea with Auntie Apple," said Libby-Ann.

"Auntie Apple?" her mother asked. "Do you mean Mrs Bramley?"

"Yes, Mama, I thought she had such lovely pink cheeks, and somehow 'Auntie Apple' suited her, her name being Bramley, which is the name of an apple, isn't it?"

Everyone laughed but had to agree it was a perfect name for their new friend.

"You must ask her politely if she minds you calling her that," Mama told Libby-Ann as they crossed the lane to the other cottage.

In fact, Mrs Bramley thought it was a huge joke and was pleased with her new name, so 'Auntie Apple' she became.

There was a wonderful spread laid out in her parlour. Not only were there freshly baked scones but jam and cream as well and also one of the very fashionable Victoria sandwich cakes. It was delicious, light as a feather!

"Well, my dears," Auntie Apple explained, "I keep my own hens, so the cake is made with fresh eggs, and that makes a difference."

"Do you keep your own cow too?" asked Elspeth. "Does it give you cream?"

"Well, what a clever girl you are!" said Auntie Apple. "I do have Buttercup, my cow, and also Naughty, my goat, who live in the back paddock. You can come and see them when you like and help me milk Buttercup. You have to watch Naughty—he'll eat anything that comes near his mouth, even the laundry off the line, if I'm not careful! That's how he got his name. He's full of mischief!"

"Can we come tomorrow?" Ernest asked his mother.

"If Auntie Apple can put up with you, then I'm sure you can. However, we must go back now and settle ourselves into our holiday home. We have three whole weeks just to have fun together!" Mama answered.

Auntie Apple loaded them up with freshly baked bread, scones, a jug of Buttercup's milk and some vegetables from her garden. "Just to get you started," she said.

The family were amazed at her kindness and friendliness, and knew they had made a new friend.

There was something special about being in the cottage. They were all living together, not separated by 'upstairs' and 'downstairs' and 'the nursery floor' as they were at home. The children loved having their mother near all the time, and Cook, Brownie and Polly were allowed to wear ordinary clothes instead of their uniforms. Of course, they were still very respectful, but they seemed more like a family.

There was so much to do and explore in those three weeks. Most days were sunny, and so the children spent lots of time out of doors. Auntie Apple became a special friend. She was a widow of many years but had always lived in Abbotsbury and knew the village history. Her children were grown up but still lived in the area, and her grandchildren came to visit, so they sometimes played with the Mountjoy Evans family. Elspeth being so young still spent most of the time with Polly, but Ernest and Libby-Ann were given a lot of freedom to explore the village as well as to learn how to milk Buttercup and hunt for eggs in Auntie Apple's garden.

One of their first adventures was to climb the hill to visit St Catherine's chapel. It was quite a climb, but from the top the children could see for miles. One aspect looked over to Chesil Beach and the Fleet, an inland lagoon behind the Chesil bank of pebbles. The hill itself was a joy to them. They took their butterfly nets with them and found so many varieties.

"Papa will be so pleased with us," said Libby-Ann. "How I wish we could write and tell him all about this wonderful place!"

"We could write a journal, and when he comes home he can read it," suggested Ernest.

"That's a brilliant idea!" enthused Libby-Ann. "We can start tonight and also put in it the bits of the Bible we are reading with Mama, 'cos it's really interesting."

"Yes, it's far more interesting than I ever imagined," agreed Ernest. "Chapel at school often seems boring, like going to church. There are so many long words, but when Mama explains it to us it seems to come alive. It makes me want to find out more about Jesus like Papa is doing. Somehow, it helps to be doing the same thing even though he is so far away."

"I know what you mean," replied his sister. "At times I get scared that he will be eaten by a lion or something else terrible will happen to him and he won't ever come home. Then I pray and ask God to bless him and look after him. That usually makes me feel better."

The children went into the tiny chapel. Auntie Apple had told them all about the chapel's story.

Around 1044, the Benedictine monks had founded a monastery in Abbotsbury. In time, six small chapels had been built in the surrounding countryside, but only St Catherine's survived. St Catherine is the patron saint of many groups of people, among them spinsters. Spinsters are unmarried ladies, and in Victorian times it was thought to be very strange for a woman not to marry.

According to legend, it was a spinster who gave the money for the chapel to be built, and she went to pray regularly that God would give her a husband. Ever since, people have travelled from far and wide to pray for good husbands!

Ernest and Libby-Ann thought that was a very interesting story, and they entered the chapel and prayed together. In Victorian Britain nobody ever went out without wearing a hat, but out of respect the men and boys took them off when they went inside a building, especially a church. Ernest removed his cap, and both children asked God to keep their father safe, and Libby-Ann told God that she didn't want a husband for a very long time!

Out in the sunshine again, the children decided to roly-poly all the way down the steep hill, trying to avoid the sheep that were quite startled by two young people rolling around them!

Chapter Eight

Some days, they all went to the beach, but not usually the village beach because the shore was made of pebbles, not sand, and then it shelved very deeply, which was dangerous for swimming. Their mother arranged for a carriage to take them to Weymouth to play on the sands. It was such fun! Auntie Apple seemed to have a huge supply of things which could be used for digging the sand, and they made castles and tunnels to their heart's content. Soon the children became very brown, even though they kept hats on and most of their clothes. Elspeth and Polly spent most of their time paddling, and even Brownie and Cook came to the beach where Brownie rolled up his trousers and paddled.

On Sunday morning, they all dressed in their best clothes and went to St Nicholas' church in Abbotsbury. Part of it was very old, dating back to the times of the monastery, and outside there were monastic ruins. Below the church they could see the large tithe barn and the road which led to the swannery. In the days of the monks, the swans were used for food, just as ducks and geese are still eaten today.

After the service, Mama took the children to visit their grandparents for luncheon. Her parents sent their carriage to collect them and drive them to their home in a village the other side of Weymouth called Sutton Poyntz.

Mama's parents seemed rather severe and expected the children to be very well behaved at all times, but especially on Sundays. The children were not allowed to go out and play or explore the village but instead had to sit in the parlour and read books or talk politely with their grandparents. It was particularly trying for Elspeth who could not read and did not have Polly around to play with her. That first Sunday afternoon, she decided to explore by herself. The grown-ups were all talking about Queen Victoria, who was still grieving very much for Prince Albert and how difficult it must be to be a queen. Ernest and Libby-Ann were quietly reading. No one noticed Elspeth slip out of the door. She somehow found her way to the back garden and was happy enough looking at the flowers. No one was around because after luncheon Grandmama's servants had been given the afternoon off, so nobody saw the little girl slip out of the back gate and wander down to the Jordan River and the millpond.

There were lots of ducks swimming in the river, and as soon as they saw Elspeth they came over to her, hoping she had some bread. They left the water and waddled up the bank and made a great deal of noise. Elspeth thought they were going to peck at her, and she began to cry and run away. Suddenly, she became very confused. She looked around and had no idea where she was. She kept running with the ducks chasing after her, but she had no idea where she was going.

In the parlour, Libby-Ann looked up from her book. She liked reading, but it was a sunny afternoon and she longed to get outside and run around, though being Sunday, she knew that wouldn't be allowed.

Suddenly, she realised that Elspeth was missing and that her picture book had been dropped on the floor.

"Excuse me, Mama," she said very politely. "Where is Elspeth?"

Grandmama looked up and frowned at her granddaughter.

"You should not interrupt our conversation. You know children should be seen and not heard, especially when you are in the parlour, Elizabeth-Ann," she scolded.

However, her mother had looked up and in alarm said, "Where is she? We must all look for her at once."

"I'm sure there is no need to panic," said Grandpapa. "You have always been too lenient with your children, Belinda. I'll look through the house and find her."

In a few minutes he returned, shaking his head and saying there was no sign of her indoors. Mama was now very worried and she, Ernest and Libby-Ann and Major the Springer Spaniel went together to search the garden. They were alarmed when they saw the back door ajar and even more so at the sight of the back gate wide open.

"I hope she didn't go down to the river or mill pond," said Mama anxiously. They searched around without any success.

"All the ducks have gone too," commented Ernest. "Whatever can have happened?"

Mama was very frightened that Elspeth may have fallen into the river or pond and drowned. She went white as a sheet at the thought.

"Mama," said Libby-Ann, "let's ask Jesus to help us. That's what people did in the gospels we've been reading."

Strange though it must have looked, they stood under the willow trees and held hands, and Mama said a simple prayer asking Jesus to look after Elspeth and for them to find her.

Straight afterwards, Ernest had a thought.

"Mama, I'll run back to the house and find her doll. Major is a gun dog. If he smells it, he will remember the scent and maybe follow the trail to Elspeth."

"What a good idea!" Mama agreed. "Run at once for the doll." Ernest was really only a few minutes getting the doll, but it seemed like hours to Mama and Libby-Ann, both of whom were crying.

Major caught the scent at once and began to sniff around and then led the way over the little bridge and up a lane, past the pumping station and up the hill. It was a long way, and everyone thought how frightened Elspeth must be. They climbed right up the hill to where the white horse was carved out of the hillside. Then, much to their relief, they found Elspeth curled up in a little ball and fast asleep, surrounded by a ring of ducks.

The ducks almost looked like a ring of angels protecting her, for they had stopped pecking and squawking and were sitting down with their heads under their wings. When Major appeared, they flew off at once back to the river.

"Elspeth, it's Mama," said her mother gently, stooping down to pick up her little daughter. Elspeth opened her eyes, and they filled with tears. She put up her arms, and a big smile came over her little face when Libby-Ann gave her the doll.

It was such a relief to know that Elspeth was safe and sound. Standing there on the white horse, they said thank you to God for leading them to her and for keeping her safe.

Once all the drama was over, Ernest saw that there were lots of butterflies on the hill. He wished he had his butterfly net with him! Maybe they could come another day to their grandparents, and he could explore this hill again. Elspeth had discovered a wonderful place for butterflies!

As they walked home, their mother told them about the white horse. It was the only chalk horse in the country, as far as she knew, that had a figure on it. It depicted King George III riding away from Weymouth.

"It wasn't because he didn't like the town, because he came back many times, and so it became well known for the lovely beaches," she told them.

As soon as they arrived back at their grandparent's house, they saw Grandpapa at the gate anxiously looking for them.

"Thank goodness all is well," he said. "Come on in. Your Grandmama is almost overcome with worry."

Although they were very strict grandparents like most Victorians, they really loved their grandchildren. Grandmama hugged them all and wiped the tears from her eyes.

"I think we all need some tea and cakes to get over the shock before you all go back to Abbotsbury," she said.

Libby-Ann was hugging Major. "You are the best dog in the world, for you found Elspeth for us!" she said, and everyone agreed.

Chapter Nine

A few days after Elspeth's adventure, Ernest asked his mother if he could go back to Sutton Poyntz on a weekday because he wanted to go butterfly hunting on the white horse hill. So it was arranged that after the family had visited on the following Sunday, Ernest would stay for a night with his grandparents and look for butterflies on the Monday. His grandfather was looking forward to spending time with Ernest too, for he didn't see him very often.

That Monday it seemed strange in the cottage without Ernest. Libby-Ann was wondering what to do when her mother decided that Polly could take Elspeth over to visit Auntie Apple while she and Libby-Ann could have time together and visit the swannery.

Libby-Ann was very excited about this. She was pleased to have her Mama all to herself and thought the swannery would be interesting. In fact, it was! Just in case she found some butterflies, she took her butterfly net with her as well, and Cook made them a small picnic.

They walked through the ruins of the old monastery of St Peter, which had been ransacked when King Henry VlIl dissolved the monasteries in 1537. Ever since then it had belonged to the local land owners, the Strangways family, but the public were allowed to walk along the footpaths. They passed the huge tithe barn.

"What does 'tithe' mean?" Libby-Ann asked her mother.

"In olden days," Mama explained, "ordinary people often did not have money to put in the offering plate at church, so instead, when their crops came in, they would give one tenth of that to God. A tithe's meaning is giving a tenth, just as the ancient Israelites were commanded to do in the Old Testament. One tenth of all they produced or earned was given to God, and the remaining nine-tenths was for their own needs. The things given to God were then used to feed the priest, or here, the monks and also the poor. Actually, it is a really good principle."

They walked through a large field, in which there were sheep and a few lambs which had grown quite large, and down to the Fleet lagoon, where the swans lived. In July and August, the swans didn't fly away because it was the time of year when they moulted their feathers. In the lagoon there was plenty of food in the mud, so they were happy to stay. Also, there were still some fluffy cygnets around.

Swans can be quite territorial, and so Mama kept hold of Libby-Ann's hand and made sure she didn't get too close to the large reed nests where many of the swans were sitting. Others were swimming on the lagoon and looked really beautiful.

"They are so beautiful," commented Libby-Ann. "How could the monks eat them?"

"They were a very good source of meat," her mother told her, "and really not so different to us eating goose at Christmas or duck occasionally. Actually, talking about ducks, I'll show you something very old."

Her mother led her through the willow trees to a long tunnel made from willow branches.

"What is that?" Libby-Ann asked.

"That is a duck decoy—a sort of trap. The monks or farmers with their hunting dogs, often spaniels like Major and Rex, would corner ducks so that they would run into the tunnels, where they could be caught for food. This has been happening since Roman times," her mama told her.

Then Libby-Ann had a good idea.

"Can I collect swan feathers to make make Indian headdresses?" she asked.

"What an excellent idea!" answered Mama, so they began to do that and found some really beautiful specimens to take away.

When they had enough, Mama suggested they go back into the field to have their picnic. "We don't want the swans to bother us," she said. "I think I heard that bread isn't good for them because it swells up in their stomach and causes problems. Anyway, I think you have had enough trouble with penguins—we don't want any more with swans!"

A little stream flowed through the field, and the trunk of a large willow tree had grown sideways, which made a lovely seat for them. They rested and ate their picnic. Mama then suggested that Libby-Ann take off her boots and stockings and paddle in the water.

It was lovely and cool, and there were newts, crayfish and tiny sticklebacks in the water. Libby-Ann wished she had a fishing net and jar to catch some and show Ernest. She wondered how many butterflies he had found—there were certainly plenty in the field and near the stream.

"Mama," she said, almost shyly, "Mama, thank you for giving me yourself all day today. I love you so much! Sometimes I think you love Ernest more than me because he is a boy and Elspeth because she is a baby still."

"Oh, my darling girl," said her mother, "come and sit with me."

Libby-Ann did as she was told. Her mother put her arm around her.

"I love you very much, as does your Papa. I love you just as much as the others, and you must never think otherwise. Yes, Elspeth does get a lot of attention, but so did you when you were small, and yes, Ernest is also special, the first and the heir, but no more special than you are. Soon you will be old enough to come with me when I have social engagements, and you will learn to live the life of a lady. I know that is hard for you now and you prefer to be outdoors and climbing trees, but one day I'm sure you'll enjoy other things too!"

"Mama," asked Libby-Ann, "would you climb the hill with me and see St Catherine's chapel? There are many butterflies on the hill, and I might catch some."

"I think I can manage that, even though it may not be very easy in this crinoline dress. It may look pretty, but it is not so good for exploring the countryside! You may have to run ahead of me!"

Up on the hill, Libby-Ann soon became absorbed in her hunt

for butterflies. She found small tortoiseshells, several fritillaries and some of her favourites from the 'Blue' family. Mama had taken a long time to climb the hill, hampered as she was by the layers of petticoats which Victorian ladies wore underneath their crinoline dresses and always having to make sure her hat was well secured by hat pins and would not blow off in the breeze! After she'd admired the butterflies, they began to walk down the other side of the hill and into the woods. Here there were many very old oak trees, and it was cool and delightful. Suddenly, Libby-Ann spotted a butterfly such as she had never seen before. It was purple! Could she catch it? Very stealthily she began to creep up on it and tried to allow it to settle so that when it did, she could pounce with her net, just as her father had taught her. She caught it! Very gently she took it to her mother and asked her what it was.

"I think it must be a Purple Emperor," said her mother. "What a find! They are not easy to see because they like to fly near the tops of trees like these oaks, but they do like to lay their eggs on willow trees, and there are plenty of those around here. I think you might have a very jealous brother!"

After all this excitement, they walked back to the cottage with their extraordinary find. Once it was safely in the 'butterfly box' which Papa had made for them, Libby-Ann and Mama made a drink before Mama went for a rest and Libby-Ann crossed the road to visit Auntie Apple and tell her all about the wonderful butterfly!

Chapter Ten

That evening, after Ernest had returned from Sutton Poyntz, everyone wanted to hear about his day.

"I had a really great time," he told them. "Grandpapa and Major went with me on the hill. I thought the dog would be a nuisance, but he wasn't bothered and didn't try to chase the butterflies at all in the way that Rex does. Grandpapa took a long time to climb the hill, but he told me to run on ahead. I found so many butterflies—afterwards we identified them together, and I have brought the best specimens home. I'll get them and show you."

Ernest had some lovely butterflies, but Libby-Ann was bursting with excitement, wanting to show him the special one which she had caught.

"Come and see mine," she said proudly. Ernest was as excited as his sister when he saw the Purple Emperor.

Then Ernest told them how Grandpapa had taken him to the pumping station at the end of the village by the Jordan River and asked the foreman if they could go inside and see the huge beam engine at work.

"The engineering is really impressive," he told them. "Grandpapa says that during the reign of our queen, England has become the world's leading industrial nation, and we are renowned for our inventions! I am really proud to be British and Victorian!

"After a luncheon of cold meat and vegetables, I went with Grandpapa into his workshop, and we made a boat together. Look at it!" Ernest showed the sailing boat they had made, and it was very splendid.

"He said that a good place to give it a maiden voyage would be Newton's Cove. It is between Weymouth and Sandsfoot Castle. Grandpapa kindly said that he would send the carriage round and we could all go there tomorrow. If you have other plans, Grandpapa told me to tell you not to worry because his groom can drive on to Bridport and get some supplies he needs. What do you think, Mama?"

"It sounds a lovely idea," Mama answered. "I wanted to take you to Sandsfoot and Castle Cove but thought we might have to get the train. How kind of Grandpapa to send the carriage. Today Libby-Ann and I collected lots of swans' feathers to make Indian headdresses, so shall we have a go before bed?"

It took all evening to make the headdresses, but they did look splendid, and Ernest and Libby-Ann decided they would play 'Cowboys and Indians' one day very soon. They had even made a little one for Elspeth and one for Polly to wear when they played together!

"I might be able to make a bow and arrow and a tomahawk," said Ernest. "Grandpapa allowed me to use his tools today when we made the boat."

"I expect that Brownie would help you," Mama said. "Maybe Auntie Apple has some tools."

After dinner it was time for the family to read together from the Bible, and the passage was from St Matthew chapter 8 where Jesus calmed the storm. The children were amazed that Jesus had power to command the wind and waves! They had seen the power of the waves on the Chesil Beach, and that was just with a brisk wind, not really in a storm. They couldn't imagine what it would be like on a really stormy day, but they knew there had been shipwrecks on the coast.

After reading, they all prayed for Papa but had no idea of the great danger he and his friends were facing!

After the three men had been captured by the pygmies, they thought their lives might come to an end. They prayed together for their families and that God would support and care for them. The biggest fear was that perhaps the pygmies were cannibals and were looking for a good meal!

However, that terrible fear was not realised. They were kept as prisoners at the settlement. The huts were strange, hollowed out into the ground so that there was as much space underground as above. Of course, the pygmies are very small people, so they had no trouble in standing upright, but it was difficult for the three men. The women in the settlement brought them food and a strange brew to drink, but the captives were so thankful for nourishment that they didn't complain. Anyway, they had no way of talking to the pygmies except through sign language, which they invented as the days went by. Their food was mainly berries and grubs which had been boiled. Always the hut where they were living was guarded by a young man with a bow, arrows and a spear. The men knew enough about the pygmy people to understand that they used poisoned tipped arrows and spears which were deadly, so they dared not try to escape.

The men of the tribe went out hunting, some during the day and others during the night. They made nets from jungle vines and hung these between bushes, then drove their prey into the nets with wild cries and strange dances. Once the animals were caught in this way, they were easily killed by poisoned arrows. The forest was not full of game, and so the mainstay of their diet was the grubs which they dug up from the forest floor as well as the beetles, locusts and flying ants along with mushrooms and fruits. For generations these little people had lived in this way in the forest and were skilled at knowing what was good to eat and what was poisonous. They also brewed up leaves and bark from some of the trees, which made a sort of bitter tea.

The days were boring for the men. They tried to listen carefully to the words which the pygmies used in order to learn their language. It was slow and hard work, but at least it kept them sane.

The men thanked God that they were together and also that none of their possessions in their rucksacks had been stolen, so they still had a Bible which they tried to read together and discuss and study. They had sketchbooks, pencils and pens, though the amount of paper was limited. None of the precious drawings of specimens which they had with them were spoilt, so they could still continue a little with their work.

They were only allowed outside the hut one at a time for trips to the loo (of course there was no such thing, but there was a place outside the camp used for these needs). They were always taken by a young guard. He seemed just a boy, maybe too young to go out on the main hunting party, but he carried a spear. The men who had been on the night hunting party were also around during the day, so there was little chance to escape.

The men were always so thankful to be able to stand upright and stretch their legs. Much to their captors' amazement and hilarity, they did exercises every time they left the hut to try to keep their muscles working properly.

Soon the pygmies became friendlier towards their prisoners and pointed to objects like a cooking pot and said 'sufaria', as if to teach the men the language they spoke.

The explorers were puzzled. If the pygmies didn't mean to kill them, why had they taken them captive? They were given as much food as the rest of the settlement. Fires were lit for them at night in the middle of the hut, keeping them warm in the mountain air and helping to keep the insects away. The days began to drift into weeks, so they had difficulty keeping track of time. Sometimes they became irritable with each other, but most of the time the three men got on well. They laughed together at the long beards which they were growing. Sometimes the pygmies laughed too and came to touch their hair and stroke their beards, which were so different from their springy, curly hair.

At times the captives became despairing. Would they ever see their families again? It didn't seem very likely. They tried to sing songs and hymns to keep themselves cheerful, but it became increasingly difficult to stay positive, even though they thanked God that he had promised never to leave them or forsake them. That promise was truly a life line!

Chapter Eleven

The children couldn't remember having had such a wonderful summer holiday before—the sun seemed to shine almost every day! Mama wanted it to be a real holiday for everyone, and she was so glad that Brownie and Cook were able to have time together to go out and walk on the hills or by the sea. She did her best to give Polly time off too, but Polly seemed to like to be with the children and play on the beach and paddle in the sea.

Grandfather's carriage arrived in the middle of the morning to take them all to Newton's Cove—a rocky inlet the other side of Weymouth Harbour—and the Nothe Fort where the soldiers were barracked. It was an interesting place with lots of rock pools and a great view of Portland, a mysterious place which was almost, but not quite, an island, although everyone called it 'the island'.

As soon as they had arrived and unloaded the picnic, fishing nets, buckets and spare clothes in case they got too wet, the children wanted to explore. Polly took Elspeth down to the rock pools to try and catch tiny crabs and shrimps, while Ernest and Libby-Ann began to climb on the rocks. It was almost impossible to keep their hats on as there was a stiff breeze blowing. Mama sat with all the belongings, looking out to sea and wondering how her husband was getting on. Something inside her was troubling her just a little, and she couldn't understand why. They had received a letter only a month ago, and very often many months went by without receiving news. She tried to dismiss the thoughts and tell herself that she was just missing her husband as she always did when he was on an expedition. Her loneliness was part of being the wife of an explorer, but at least she had the children and this wonderful time with them on holiday! What was the hymn they sang in church last Sunday—wasn't it, 'Count your blessings, name them one by one'? She should remember to do that.

"Look Libby-Ann," remarked Ernest, "isn't that a strange rock? It's quite different from all the rest."

Libby-Ann climbed down to the shore where her brother was peering at a small rock. It was indeed a different colour to the other rocks around and had a shiny appearance. They lifted it up and examined it. Their father had taught them to be curious and observe the world around them.

"I wonder what it is?" questioned Libby-Ann. "Do you think it might be a fossil? This coast is famous for such things."

"Well, it might be," answered Ernest thoughtfully, "but I can't see any obvious shapes like shells or leaves on it. Don't fossils come in ordinary rocks anyway? This is brown and shiny."

"Let's take it to Mama. She might know," suggested Libby-Ann.

The rock wasn't very big, and Ernest could easily pick it up and carry it. They clambered over the cliffs back to their mother.

"Mama," Ernest asked, "have you any idea what this rock is

called? It seems quite unusual."

She looked at it carefully and agreed that it was unusual. "Let me think for a few moments," she told the children. "I have something in the back of my mind but can't quite recall it. Your Papa told me once about some special rocks."

They sat by their Mama watching the sailing boats, and it reminded Ernest that he was going to sail his little boat. They went off and found a big rock pool and had great fun sailing it from one side to the other before Mama called them all to return for the picnic.

"Why does food taste so much better out of doors?" asked Libby-Ann.

Mama laughed. "I don't know, but it obviously does, because you all eat everything which Cook has packed! I shall have to get Polly to let out all the seams in your clothes when we get home!" Polly just grinned at this—she was loving being on the first holiday she had ever had.

They packed up all their belongings, ready to walk together to Sandsfoot Castle. Grandpapa's groom was to meet them there later that afternoon. Ernest picked up his precious rock, but at that moment he actually didn't realise that it was indeed very precious!

Sandsfoot Castle was an interesting ruin, and for a while the two older children played a battle game inside the ramparts. From the castle there was a wonderful view all over Portland Harbour and to the island, where another castle faced them. Their mother told them that King Henry VIII had built the castles to defend the coastline and make the country secure from invasion.

"The same king as the one who'd had the monastery broken down and stole all it treasures?" asked Libby-Ann.

"Yes, the very same king," her mother replied. "And by the way, children," she said to Ernest and Libby-Ann, "about that rock— I have remembered what your Papa said. I think it may be called ambergris. If it is that, then it is highly sought after by perfumers who use it in making expensive perfumes. We'll take it home and have it examined."

The family were sitting on a grassy mound which had once been the edge of the moat around the castle. Several other people were doing the same, enjoying the afternoon sunshine, including a couple of lads who were probably in their late teens. These boys were sitting behind the Mountjoy Evans family, so they didn't notice when the boys sat up and looked meaningfully at each other as they overheard what Mama was saying.

"Can we go down to the sands?" asked Elspeth. Mama agreed, so they packed up their belongings and walked a little way down the lane, then down many wooden steps to Castle Cove, a lovely little sandy beach with an old wrecked ship stranded on the shore. It was a great place to play. There were also some very pretty little shells which Libby-Ann decided to collect. While she was doing that, Ernest took his little boat to the shore, and before too long the older lads came alongside and chatted.

"That's a nice boat," one commented.

"Yes, I made it with my grandpapa yesterday," he replied, "and it sails really well."

"Can I have a go?" asked one of the lads. Not suspecting anything, Ernest agreed. The boy paddled out and took the boat much further from the shore than Ernest had done.

"Please don't go too far," pleaded Ernest. "I don't want to lose it!"

"If you want me to give it back, then you'll have to do a swap!" said the lad. He sounded like the big boys at school who sometimes bullied the younger ones. Ernest didn't quite know what to think or do. He knew at school it would never do to show you were afraid and certainly not to run to an adult, but he felt very worried.

"Tell you what, why don't you give me that old brown bit of rock you had by the castle," suggested the lad, and the other big boy agreed. "That would be a good swap—it's only an old stone after all!"

Warning bells sounded in Ernest's mind. His mother had said it might be precious. He wasn't about to give it up. He might just let the boys have his boat.

"No way," he answered. "My papa is an explorer and I'm keeping it to show him. If you must, keep my boat."

The bigger lads looked at each other. "We don't want your boat," one told him. "We were just teasing you. We haven't seen you before. Do you live here?"

Ernest, relieved that he wouldn't lose either his boat or his rock, thought maybe they just wanted to be friendly.

"No, I live in Addiscombe, Croydon. That's south of London," he explained as the boys looked a bit puzzled. He could tell by their accents that they were local boys.

"We're on holiday, staying in a cottage in Abbotsbury," he added, trying to be polite and friendly.

"That sounds nice," said the other boy. "Sometimes we go fishing on the Fleet. It's a nice village. Where are you staying?"

"At Honeysuckle Cottage on Rodden Row," Ernest told them, and the boys looked at each other knowingly as they handed him back his little boat.

"See you, then," one of them said. "Enjoy the rest of your holiday."

Ernest went back to this mother and sisters and forgot all about the encounter. They began to pack up all their things, and he carried his precious rock and boat all the way up the wooden steps to the lane, where the carriage was waiting for them. It had been such a fantastic day, and they all were happy and tired and ready to go home.

Chapter Twelve

That evening the family had been invited to have an evening meal with Auntie Apple. She was such a lovely old lady, and everyone had become very fond of her. Once, many years ago, she had been the school teacher in the Abbotsbury school. She knew so many things, especially about the countryside and the coastline around the village. Ernest took his special rock with him to show her.

"Oh Ernest," she exclaimed, "this is such an exciting find. It's almost like finding a treasure trove!"

Auntie Apple held the piece of rock with great care and gently ran her hands over it.

"Do you know what it is?" she asked.

Mama told her that she thought it might be ambergris, which she once heard her husband mention but could not remember much about it.

"Very occasionally a fisherman will find a piece floating on the sea, but more often it is picked up on the rocks. It has been vomited up by a sperm whale. Strangely, it is produced in the intestines of the sperm whale. It seems that when they have something they just cannot digest, the whale then coats it with some sort of substance and vomits it up. It takes years to form around the foreign body and may float for years before becoming hard enough to be left on the rocks. The name comes from French. 'Gris' means grey—so it is grey amber. When it is first formed, it is rather like faeces—the poo of the whale, but as it ages it becomes sweeter and is very valuable because perfumers use it as a fixative in perfumes to make the smell last longer. You have really found a sea treasure that may be worth hundreds, if not thousands, of pounds!"

Everyone looked amazed and shocked when they heard this. It really was as good as finding buried treasure!

"What shall we do with it?" asked Ernest.

"When you get back to London, it should be taken to one of the high-class perfumers. Don't just sell it to any Tom, Dick or Harry," Auntie Apple advised them. "Meanwhile, look after it well. There are always people who beachcomb the area and who are on the lookout for such treasure."

They had a lovely time with Auntie Apple, who sent them home with newly-laid eggs and another jug of milk from Buttercup.

"I shall miss you all when you go home," she told them, and the family all told her how much they would miss her too.

"We can write to you and tell you our news, can't we?" asked Libby-Ann.

"I would love that, dear," she answered, "and perhaps you can come back next year!"

"Maybe Papa will be home then and he can come too!" Elspeth

added sleepily, for it was past her bedtime.

That evening Ernest thought over what Auntie Apple had said about the ambergris. Maybe the two big boys who wanted him to give it to them were beachcombers and knew its value. He had told them where they were staying. Would they try to steal it? It was a horrible thought.

Before he went to sleep, he knelt to pray and asked God to keep the ambergris safe and watch over all of them, including Papa and Papa's sister and her family. He climbed into bed and tried to sleep but kept thinking about the ambergris. A thought was in his head and would not go away. He should hide it in an unlikely place until they went home. The only unlikely place he could think about was the outhouse—the loo at the bottom of the garden. At night the family didn't usually go outside but used chamber pots, but Ernest decided to wrap the precious rock in an old shirt and take it down the garden and hide it. He crept downstairs, not wanting to disturb anyone, unlocked the back door and lifted the latch. It was dark and cold, with the wind howling off the sea. He thought of Jesus calming the storm and asked him to keep the rock safe. Suddenly, he had a thought which made him laugh. "The ambergris is left in the right place. Where else would you leave sperm whale poo?"

Once he had completed his task, he locked the door and went to bed, feeling much happier. Very quickly he went to sleep.

The next day was wet, and so the children played in the cottage most of the morning. They also wrote long letters to their papa, which would be sent to the society in London that had sponsored the expedition to the Congo, just in case someone was going out who could take them. After luncheon the skies cleared, and Mama and the two older children went for a walk, while Polly took Elspeth to see Naughty the goat and Buttercup the cow. Auntie Apple had promised to show Polly how to make butter from the cream of the milk. All these things were new to Polly, who had always lived in a town, so she was very excited.

Ernest and Libby-Ann asked their mother if they could go to the Abbotsbury beach. It was about a mile's walk from the main village, but they enjoyed walking down the pretty lane and then spent a long time looking for tiny shells among the shingle of the beach. They found some fish eggshells which were interesting, and they decided to add them to their collection as well as some pieces of cuttlefish shell which Mama told them Rafiki their parrot would like.

"Birds like to sharpen their beaks on it," she explained.

"We'll have to watch out then," remarked Libby-Ann. "He might bite our fingers!"

Rafiki was an African grey parrot. Their Papa had brought it back from one of his earlier trips. He was a good mimic and copied many things they said but also sometimes said things in Swahili, the East African trade language that had been spoken around him many years ago. It was amazing how good his memory was!

"Let's go hunting for more cuttlefish shells for him," suggested Ernest.

"You can," replied Libby-Ann, "but I'm going to stay with Mama and keep her company."

Ernest wandered off on his own. He was near the shore when he heard the oars of a rowing boat. He looked around and saw two young men rowing to the shore. As they came nearer, Ernest recognised them—they were the boys who had taken his boat the day before.

"Well, well!" one of them said. "Fancy meeting you again! Just the boy we want! We were coming to find you, but you have made it easy for us. We want you to hand over the rock you found yesterday!"

"I don't have it," said Ernest, truthfully. "And even if I did, I wouldn't give it to you." He spoke as boldly as he could but was shaking inside.

"Wouldn't you now?" replied the other boy in a nasty voice, and he pulled out a sharp knife such as fishermen used to gut the fish they had caught. He grabbed Ernest and held the knife to his throat. "You will do as we ask and give us the rock!"

Ernest began to call out 'Help!' to his mother, but the roar of the sea and the sound it made as it sucked the shingle away made his cry inaudible to the others who were up on the beach.

"Get into the boat," he was told, and because of the knife, Ernest did as he was told. Fear rose up in him, and he felt sick.

"Where are you taking me?" he tried to ask, as one boy managed the oars while the other held the knife dangerously near his neck.

"You'll see," he was told. The young man rowed hard against the tide and round the coast to the Fleet and the other end of Abbotsbury.

Meanwhile, because Ernest had been gone for such a long time, Mama sent Libby-Ann to get him, because they ought to be making their way back to the cottage. They were leaving the next day and needed to pack their trunks.

Libby-Ann ran up and down the shingle bank and looked all along the shore. There was no sign of her brother anywhere. She found a mound of cuttlefish shells, which looked as if they had been dropped in a hurry. She picked them up and ran along the shoreline one way and then the other, calling for Ernest. Something made her feel a bit scared, for Ernest was not as impulsive as she was and didn't get into trouble for running off and things like that. In the end, very breathless, she appeared over the shingle mound and ran to her Mama with the bad news that she couldn't find Ernest.

Then Mama began to get worried as well, and so together they searched and called, but all in vain. It seemed he had disappeared into thin air! There were no cliffs or rocks where he could have fallen or hidden. It was just a long shingle beach and then the sea. Surely he couldn't have been washed out to sea! The horror of that thought made Mama cry, and Libby-Ann joined her.

"This won't do," sniffed Mama. "We need to be brave and sensible. He can't be far away. We must walk back to the village and get help. He is a big boy and quite able to find his way home too. Maybe he walked too far in one direction and will walk up to the village by another path."

Libby-Ann felt a bit relieved to hear her mother say that. Even so, she had another idea.

"Before we start for home, why don't we ask Jesus to find Ernest. He found the lost sheep and he knows where we all are, doesn't he?"

"Yes dear," said her mother and held her daughter close to her while she asked the Lord to help them find Ernest and to take care of him.

After they had prayed, somehow Libby-Ann no longer felt afraid. If Jesus was alive as the Bible taught them and was the same person as he had been when he lived all those years ago, then he could find her brother. She took her Mama's hand and squeezed it.

"Everything will be fine, Mama. We can trust Jesus to help," she said as they began the long walk back to the cottage.

There were very few people around, but Mama asked everyone they met if they had seen an eleven-year-old boy in a sailor suit during the last hour. Nobody had.

Chapter Thirteen

The boys rowed the boat onto the shore at the swannery. The one boy kept hold of Ernest, while the other pulled the boat up the beach and secured it. The swans were noisy, but the boys walked through them and into the field where Libby-Ann and Mama had eaten their picnic a couple of days previously.

"Now, act normally," said the boy with the knife. "We don't want to harm you, but we will if you do anything silly. Take us to your cottage and give us the rock. Then we will disappear."

Ernest nodded and allowed the one boy to lead the way, while the other went behind him with the knife hidden in case they were seen but near enough to Ernest's back for the boy to know that he was in danger. In his head, Ernest was praying too. God had helped him to confess when he had stolen treasure. Now he asked for help because he had found treasure and these boys wanted to steal it.

They reached the tithe barn and began to climb a small hill towards the ruins of the abbey and the parish church. They passed several cottages and made their way into the main part of the village. As they walked in one direction, Libby-Ann and Mama were almost running into the village from the other direction. Mama saw the boys and was sure the middle boy was Ernest. It was odd to see three boys in a line, one behind each other and she was sure that her son, in the middle, was in trouble. Mama motioned to Libby-Ann to slow down and be quiet. As the boys turned into Rodden Row, she went into the nearest cottage to ask for help.

"I need a policeman," she explained, "and very urgently. My son is in danger."

"The nearest police house is Portesham; that's the next village," said the housewife of the cottage. "But my Jack is in the garden. He'll go with you, I'm sure."

Jack quickly grabbed a pitchfork and hurried with Mrs Mountjoy Evans and Libby-Ann back to Honeysuckle Cottage.

Inside the kitchen was Ernest, held at knife point by one boy, and the other was questioning him.

"Where is it?" he was shouting. "We will take this house apart brick by brick until we find it!"

Ernest looked white and scared. "I'm telling you the truth that it isn't here."

"It has to be! Take us to your bedroom. You must have it hidden there."

Suddenly, Jack burst in through the door, making a lot of noise and shouting, "Might have known it was you two, the Blake boys, up to trouble again! Drop that knife at once! You harm that boy and I'll have the constabulary after you. Everyone will be glad to see you both locked up or deported to some faraway colony for the rest of your lives." With that, Jack rushed towards the boys with his pitchfork held in a very menacing way. He knew that these boys were thieves and also bullies and cowards.

"We wouldn't have harmed him—we just want a rock he found on the beach. You know us beachcombers—we take a fancy to things," said one of the Blake boys, handing over the knife to Jack, who was a huge figure of a man and not one to argue with!

At that moment, Brownie and Cook appeared. They had been visiting Auntie Apple and arrived back to see a strange scene in the kitchen.

"Whatever is happening in my kitchen?" asked Cook, grabbing her rolling pin and looking just as dangerous as Jack!

"These two boys, ma'am," Jack said. "They are thugs from Weymouth, well known for causing trouble, and now I've caught them red-handed menacing a knife at the young master. I've a good mind to march them down to the constabulary in Portesham. They'll get their just deserts!"

"I'll help you," said Brownie. "I'll get some rope, and we can tie them up!"

"We didn't mean to hurt him! We are sorry," cried one of the boys. "Please don't hand us in to the constable. We may get hung or imprisoned for years or deported. Think of our poor ma. What would she do?"

Jack wanted to really scare the boys, but they were only boys, and he knew if he handed them in they could be severely punished. He hated the way some minor criminals were treated. He knew these

Blake boys had no pa to keep them in order. He had run off years ago, leaving their mother to cope as best she could.

"Where is that boat of yours?" Jack asked.

"At the swannery," replied the boys.

"Alright," announced Jack. "You'll help me, sir?" he asked Brownie. "We'll tie these lads up. When we are marching down the road, I will think on whether we go to Portesham constabulary or to the boat." Secretly, he had already made up his mind to let the boys go free with a warning. At the swannery, they were put into their boat and sent home. They promised never to do such a thing again, but who knows if they kept their promise?

When Jack and Brownie arrived back at Honeysuckle Cottage, the tea was brewing and Cook had managed to produce some scones, strawberry jam and cream. How grateful everyone was that all had ended well.

"I told the truth," explained Ernest. "The ambergris is not in the cottage. After I had prayed for protection last night, I felt I had to hide it somewhere safe. It is in the toilet hidden in a corner, wrapped in my shirt. After all, Auntie Apple told us that it was sperm whale poo!"

The whole story of finding the ambergris was explained to Jack, who was then thanked very much for all his help.

"I can't help feeling a bit sorry for those lads," he told them all. "You see, their pa disappeared when they were quite young, and their ma never was a strong woman, and she struggled a lot to bring them up and keep them out of the workhouse. I hope this has taught them a lesson. I'd hate to see them swing for what they tried to do."

"I have always said that a boy needs his father," remarked Mama. "It makes me hope that my husband will soon come home to his family, at least for a while. He's in the Congo looking for butterflies. I guess he'll always be an adventurer, but my boy still needs his father!"

"All's well that ends well, is what I always say," commented Cook. "You had better go and retrieve your rock, Master Ernest, while I prepare the dinner. Everyone out of my kitchen, please," she announced, waving her rolling pin menacingly again but this time making everyone laugh.

"We must all start to pack up our belongings, for we begin our journey home straight after breakfast tomorrow," Mama reminded them all.

"It's been a wonderful holiday," said Libby-Ann. "We've had so many adventures!"

"Almost too many for me," answered her mother. "I think I need to go home for a rest!"

Chapter Fourteen

Once back in Addiscombe, life seemed very tame after the wonderful summer holiday. Constance had looked after the house, and it was very nice to be reunited with Rex and Rafiki, but to return to living on the nursery floor and only having the garden in which to play seemed very restrictive to Ernest and Libby-Ann. They wrote up their nature notes on the butterflies that they had caught, with the Purple Emperor taking pride of place, and although he didn't say much, Ernest was a little jealous that his sister had found it!

Sometimes they played cowboys and Indians in the garden, and Brownie joined in when he wasn't too busy with his duties. He made the children a wigwam, which made the games more fun, and as Ernest hadn't managed to make a tomahawk or bow and arrows in Abbotsbury, he also helped Brownie with that.

It was almost time for Ernest to return to school, and he found he was quite looking forward to it, especially as he thought about all the stories he would have to share with his friend Simon. He hoped that he had also had a good holiday with lots of adventures.

They had been home a few days when Mama announced that she would take Ernest and Libby-Ann to London. She wanted Ernest to take his ambergris to a perfumer in Bond Street to have it assessed.

If it truly was a treasure, then something should be done about it. Mrs Mountjoy Evans felt a little inexperienced to do this, so she had consulted a family friend whose husband worked in central London and who knew about such things. He had promised to meet the family and escort them to the perfumer, making sure they were not cheated.

So once again Brownie drove them to Addiscombe Station where they took the train to Victoria station, this time Ernest carrying his precious rock in a rucksack on his back. This time too, Libby-Ann had promised that she would not run off anywhere on her own but hold her Mama's hand!

They had the whole morning to explore some of the London sights, so they went to look at Buckingham Palace. It was guarded by soldiers who marched up and down and looked really smart in their red coats and busby helmets! The palace was very impressive. As they stood looking at it, the main gates were opened and a carriage drove out. Libby-Ann hoped that it might have Queen Victoria inside, but Mama explained that the Queen and her family were on holiday in Scotland at Balmoral Palace. She pointed to the flag post on the palace roof and told them that if the Queen was in residence, then it would be flying the Royal Standard flag. Queen Victoria was the first sovereign to take up residence in the palace, although her uncle, King George IV, had had it all renovated and modernised.

They walked together up the mall and to Trafalgar Square and looked at Nelson on top of the column which had been built by King George IV to celebrate Nelson's great sea battle and victory at Trafalgar.

The family then took a horse-drawn omnibus and rode to the Palace of Westminster to see the Houses of Parliament and Westminster Abbey. There was so much to see and learn about that by the end of their tour they were hot, tired and thirsty, so Mama took them to a restaurant to eat luncheon.

They felt very grown up eating with her. The waiters treated them as if they were grown-ups, shaking out snowy white napkins and placing them on their laps and calling them 'sir' and 'ma'am' as they were served.

Afterwards they met their neighbour, who was to accompany them to the perfumer. Libby-Ann was excited, but Ernest found his tummy was turning over and over, and he felt slightly sick. He was thinking, "What if we are all wrong and it is a worthless rock? How stupid we will all appear." Then seconds later he was thinking, "What if it really is worth a lot of money? Will it make me rich for ever?"

Soon he was put out of his agony of worrying. They were led upstairs to a kind of laboratory where the perfumer was at work, mixing all sorts of things in tiny bottles using glass straws.

He smiled as they entered and told them to sit down and show him the ambergris.

Ernest produced it from his rucksack and carefully handed it to the perfumer. As he took it, his eyes lit up, and Ernest knew that it was the real thing. Auntie Apple had been right!

"Well, what is your opinion?" asked their neighbour. "I am

representing the family as their father is in the Congo on an important scientific expedition."

"There is no doubt that this is ambergris and a good-sized find. I will weigh it and give you the current value in pounds, shillings and pence. Here is a paper which will confirm the price per ounce, so you will know that in no way am I trying to cheat you." Then the perfumer handed a piece of paper to their neighbour.

Having weighed the ambergris, he calculated the cost, and it was indeed enormous! It was a small fortune, and Mama was shocked and turned a little pale.

"Madam," said the perfumer, "I think you may need the use of this." And he handed Mama a bottle containing smelling salts, which Victorian ladies used if they felt faint. Mama took a sniff at the bottle, and her colour returned.

"Thank you for coming to see me. I would be most grateful if you would sell this ambergris to me, young sir, and I will write a money cheque for you. I suggest you have the bank look after it for you. It is safer that way."

"Yes, sir," said Ernest in excitement. He was rich!

After they had left the perfumer, they went at once to the Bank of England in Threadneedle Street to deal with the money. There it was lodged safely in Mama's name until Ernest reached the age of twenty-one years, which was deemed the right age for him to be able to take care of it himself.

Their neighbour left them once that had been done, and they all thanked him very much for his help.

"I am so grateful to you," said Mama. "A boy needs his father to help him, but he is so far away!"

"I'm glad to have been of help, Mrs Mountjoy Evans," he answered, lifting his hat. "Anytime you need the advice of a man, if I am available, I will do my best to help."

In the train on the way home, Ernest was strangely quiet. Libby-Ann had been chatting away as usual about everything they had done through the day, but Ernest was lost in thought.

"A penny for them!" said his Mama. "What are you thinking about?" she asked her son.

"This holiday has been such a mixture, Mama. I saw the gold sovereign and stole it, thinking I had a great treasure and could buy sweets to make the school bullies like me. Then I felt so ashamed, and it only got better when I told the miller about my theft and gave the money back, but I felt sad about losing the treasure. Who could have dreamt that on the beach I would find a far greater treasure and that it was legally mine and now I am rich! Finding the ambergris made me stand up to the bullies who tried to steal it, and although I was frightened, all these things have taught me to trust in God and to pray about everything and that Jesus is with me and will help me. I'm not so afraid about going back to school and facing the bullies there. They always bully the 'small fry', as they call us."

"We have Papa to thank for so much this holiday," Mama said, thoughtfully. "His letter asking us to read the Bible and get to know

Jesus in a real, personal way has begun to change my life. I know it was Jesus who gave me thoughts to take you all to the Zoological Gardens and then to the cottage for a holiday. I believe that we are all on a very exciting journey learning to love God, Papa in the Congo, us here, and you will continue when you get back to school next week. Sometimes I worry about what I would do if anything happened to Papa while he is on an expedition, but this holiday I have learnt that we are all in God's hands and that he is strong enough to look after us all!"

So the family arrived back at Addiscombe station after another very exciting day, full of things to tell Brownie as he drove them home and with many more things to add to the letter to their Papa, which they hoped would one day reach him.

Many months later, far, far away, their Papa opened a packet from England and began to read the letters from his wife and two eldest children. His youngest daughter had drawn him a picture of a butterfly. It seemed his love of butterflies had affected all his family! He smiled and showed it to his friends. How he longed to see them all again! Would that ever happen? That is another story!